ENCOURAGING LEARNING

ENCOURAGING LEARNING

Towards a theory
of the learning school

Jon Nixon
Jane Martin
Penny McKeown
Stewart Ranson

OPEN UNIVERSITY PRESS
Buckingham • Philadelphia

Open University Press
Celtic Court
22 Ballmoor
Buckingham
MK18 1XW

and

1900 Frost Road, Suite 101
Bristol, PA 19007, USA

First Published 1996

A catalogue record of this book is available from the British Library

ISBN   0 335 19087 1 (pb)   0 335 19088 X (pb)

Library of Congress Cataloging-in-Publication Data
Encouraging learning: towards a theory of the learning school /
Jon Nixon . . . [et al.].
p.   cm.
Includes bibliographical references and index.
ISBN 0–335–19088–X, — ISBN 0–335–19087–1 (pbk.)
1. Learning.   2. Educational change—Great Britain.   I. Nixon,
Jon.
LB1060.E53   1995
370.15′23—dc20
95–9573   CIP

Typeset by Graphicraft Typesetters Ltd, Hong Kong
Printed in Great Britain by St Edmundsbury Press Ltd,
Bury St Edmunds, Suffolk

Contents

Preface

The nation's anxiety about the quality of learning in schools continues despite a decade or more of exhausting reform. Not only has the Government, through the Dearing Report, rewritten after only five years its most radical creation – the National Curriculum – but a series of reports have recently called for further reform based upon a more enriching vision of the future of education. The most significant is *Learning to Succeed*, published by the National Commission on Education (1993a). There is, arguably, a growing realization that the agenda of the recent past has failed to address not only the continuing sore of underachievement but also the fundamental questions of what the purposes of education are to be in a period of manifest structural change. The problems of 'the service', therefore, cannot be understood independently of the deeper crisis in society. For we are living through one of those historic periods of change that alter the structure of experience and, as a result, the capacities each person needs to flourish and the relationships that will be needed to sustain autonomy and collective well-being.

The quality of our future will depend upon our capacity to learn. Only if learning is placed at the centre of our experience will individuals continue to develop their capacities, institutions be enabled to respond openly and imaginatively to change, and the differences within and between communities become a source for reflective understanding. A new vision for education is needed to express the value of and conditions for a learning society.

Such a society will recover the *agency* of the learner as the key to personal and social development. We learn when we have a sense of purpose and such motivation is best likely to grow out of our active participation in creating the projects which are to shape our selves as well as the communities in which we live. Such a perspective emphasizes our dual responsibility as citizens for making our private and public worlds and that our mutual dependence and accountability are best supported through the deliberative processes of democratic decision-making. We learn about ourselves and others through deliberating with others and reasoning practically about change.

Our argument is that if society is to address seriously the problems facing education then the solution requires more than a quantitative expansion or a mere adaptation of existing systems. Rather it will need a reform of the organizing principles of learning: from an instrumental purpose – supporting the needs of the labour market and economic regeneration – to the moral and political purpose of cultural renewal; from learning for economic interest to learning for citizenship. Encouraging learning will be most effective when it grows out of an education which enables people, individually and together, to find themselves through making their communities.

This book has developed from a sustained discussion between Martin, McKeown, Nixon and Ranson in the context of the ESRC-funded project, New Forms of Education Management, and presents the early ideas and conceptual frameworks that are helping to guide that enquiry. This discussion has drawn upon and developed Ranson's work *Towards the Learning Society* (1992, 1994) and the arguments in the book are illustrated by material drawn from his studies of LEAs and from Nixon's research on Expectations in the Early Years of Secondary Schooling and Beyond, sponsored by British Petroleum.

We would like to thank ESRC and British Petroleum, especially Brian Palmer, for their support for this work. We are particularly grateful to Jean Rudduck whose patience and encouragement have made this book possible.

ONE

The limits of the present reform agendas

Education in England and Wales has for over a decade been the focus of continuous Government review and legislative change that strives to introduce the most complete reworking of the service since the 1944 Education Act. This project of education reform has been predicated on assumptions about the poor standards of teaching and learning in our schools which, it is claimed, have their roots in the mistaken project of post-war social democracy. That project, in its education form – the pursuit of equality of opportunity, through comprehensive schools and colleges, conceived of as a whole system, a seamless web of progressive learning and opportunity, and planned by local education authorities through their professional communities – was held to be responsible for the purported low expectations of teachers and schools and the underachievement of their pupils. A different vision of a consumer democracy – based upon individual choice and competition – has been promoted to replace the supposed failures of the social democratic state which lasted for a generation and more into the 1970s. The legislation since 1980 has been designed not only to alter the purpose and organization of learning but to do so as the significant part of a broader reconstituting of the polity.

Some of the Government's reforms have gained support amongst the profession and the community: for example, the need to create a national framework for the curriculum, or to focus more rigorously on the quality of learning, or to delegate more decision-making capacity to schools. Arguably, however, other aspects of policy can only frustrate the learning opportunities of most young people; principally, the trend to accord primacy to the market will only fragment local communities while centralized power engenders inertia.

The failure of the Government's reform agenda has renewed the search for a more adequate analysis of the achievements as well as the dilemmas facing education and has also led to a number of significant attempts to produce an alternative agenda for reform. These programmes too, it will be argued, have serious limitations because ultimately they fail to develop an analysis of the fundamental issues facing education in a period of social transformation. The chapter will conclude with our own framework of analysis for understanding the practices, institutional forms and social structures of learning.

The Government's reform agenda

The 1988 Education Reform Act (ERA), it was claimed, would enhance learning and achievement, improve school management and empower parents. The agenda for reforming education revolved around a number of key strategies. First, establishing a National Curriculum would provide an entitlement to broad and balanced learning for all 5- to 16-year-olds and would improve achievement by providing a better definition of what is to be taught and learned. Clearer assessment of what has been achieved would enable planned progression from stage to stage of the learning process. Such close monitoring of progress in learning would enable parents to know more clearly what was being studied, what objectives were being set and what was achieved individually and collectively. Second, better management and a better curriculum go hand in hand, and the 1988 reforms sought to create local management of schools which would allow them flexibility to use resources more effectively to respond to learning needs as articulated by the governors and parents as well as the teachers.

The quality of learning and achievement would also be improved considerably, the Government believed, if the dynamic of competition was introduced into the education system. If one school could not improve standards of achievement then parents should be able to transfer their child to another. Parents, provided with 'performance data', on examination results for example, could then make informed choices of school. By replacing the artificial planning of admissions (with open enrolment) and the resourcing of schools (with formula funding so that each pupil becomes a resource voucher) the Government sought to introduce into the school system the conditions for market competition.

The strategy of increasing the planning of learning and the opportunity for market choice of institutions could be interpreted as mutually reinforcing and designed to weaken the hold of the educational professionals: thus, the State would assume control of the internal processes of education to create (albeit equal access to) a conservative curriculum beyond the control of the teachers, while the frameworks for learning (the schools) would be placed in the market-place, beyond the control of local administrators, to ensure the virtues of competition and choice.

Although the ERA redefined responsibilities, both centralizing and devolving powers, so as potentially to undermine the local education authorities (LEAs), the law could equally be interpreted to accord the LEAs a significant but different role in the reform programme. The challenge for the new-style LEA was to set aside its traditional commitment to controlling the routine administration of local education and to concentrate instead on clarifying strategy, supporting and assuring quality in schools and colleges. A 'providing' authority was to give way to an 'enabling' authority. A plural system of education governance was, therefore, maintained but authority redistributed within an integrated but devolved framework of institutional management for post- as well as pre-16 local education.

By 1991 the policy agenda appeared to be subject to radical revision in a series of legislative proposals and altered priorities that began to unfold during 1992: in March the Education (Schools) Act 1992 (which privatized school inspections) and the Further and Higher Education Act 1992 (which nationalized further education) received the Royal Assent and in July the White Paper *Choice and Diversity: A New Framework for Schools* (DFE 1992) was published (promoting the movement of all schools to grant-maintained self-governance and thus threatening the future of the LEA). This became the Education Act 1993, the year in which the Queen's Speech proposed the restructuring of initial teacher training. A more traditional paradigm of learning was being revealed.

Back to a basic learning

Although there is the semblance of continuity between 1988 and 1992 there is actually a fundamental shift of policy. In place of 'progression', 'entitlement' and 'local management' is substituted a new emphasis upon 'standards', 'specialization', 'selection' and 'autonomy'. In the forward to *Choice and Diversity*, the Prime Minister said that 'the drive for higher standards in schools has been the hallmark

of the Government over the last decade' and was now to' be carried
forward. The White Paper emphasized that the Government was
'absolutely committed to testing . . . as the key to monitoring and
raising standards in our schools' (DFE 1992:9).

The White Paper reinforced other Government announcements
about standards. The proportion of course work in GCSE had been
reduced while that of examinations had been increased. The concern about standards in GCSE was reiterated following the publication of examination results in August 1992. A subsequent confidential
report from inspectors claimed a decline in standards and prompted
the Secretary of State to announce a review of marking. In earlier
years simpler tests are being introduced to assess a more basic curriculum. Standard attainment tasks (SATs) have been simplified with
an increase in pencil and paper tests, and some of the key curriculum orders are being reviewed. Only three years after publishing
its Orders on the teaching of English, the Government announced
a review of the subject. The traditional 'basics' were to be reinforced
with greater emphasis given to spelling, grammar and to the speaking of standard English. In October 1992 the Prime Minister on the
radio emphasized the importance of teaching facts in history.

What was emerging fitfully but surely from speeches, announcements and reviews was a different conception of learning: a move
away from an emphasis upon progression in understanding, skills
and capacity that took into account the needs of the child as a
whole person as well as the requirements of learning through the
National Curriculum. The move towards a basic standards model of
the curriculum entrenches even more securely than the subject-
based National Curriculum a conception of learning as the acquisi-
tion of separate bodies of knowledge and of assessment as selection.
It reinforces a notion of fixed levels of ability, the 'normal curve' of
achievement, and of different types of aptitude and ability: difference defined as fixed and finite and inescapably lodged within the
predetermined capabilities of the individual.

The specificity of the National Curriculum and the overload caused
by the testing and assessment system reached a crisis in 1993. What
began as a protest by English teachers over ill-prepared tests in the
subject for 14-year-olds rapidly became a boycott, whereby most
of the teaching profession refused to set, administer or mark tests
produced by the Schools Examination and Assessment Council for
14-year-olds across the subjects of the National Curriculum. This
boycott was upheld by the Appeal Court and appeared to have wide
public support. What was a particular dispute became a general
dispute about the National Curriculum, testing and in particular

the preoccupation with using information from the tests to create national league tables of school performance.

In April 1993 the Secretary of State invited Sir Ron Dearing, Chairman-designate of the new School Curriculum and Assessment Authority (SCAA) to review the manageability of the National Curriculum and testing system. The review would include the scope of the curriculum, the ten-level scale for graduating children's attainments, the complexity of the testing arrangements. Dearing, publishing an interim report in July 1993 (Dearing 1993) and a final report in January 1994 (Dearing 1994), acknowledged that while the principle of the National Curriculum had wide support, teachers were experiencing many problems in trying to implement the ERA reforms:

- curriculum overload: the sum of the individual subjects accounts for virtually the whole of the teaching time available, leaving little time to pursue curriculum objectives outside the National Curriculum or to explore links between subjects across the curriculum
- lack of training: many primary teachers did not possess the academic specialist training required by a very academic National Curriculum
- the pace of change: short lead times for implementation and the late arrival of key documents exacerbated teacher anxiety; consequently, required teaching resources were often not prepared in time
- over prescription: higher than most west European countries and seriously limiting the proper exercise of professional judgement
- bureaucratic complexity: for example, a classroom teacher at key stage 1 with 35 pupils assessing all the class against all the statements of attainment would make and record some 8,000 judgements!
- deep concern about the confused purposes of assessment: whether it was supposed to benefit the pupil in diagnosing personal needs, the teacher and school in planning the curriculum, or parents in making competitive choices of school.

In proposing to address the issues of curriculum overload, prescription and administrative burden Dearing appeared to bargain a compromise between the teachers and a New Right Government: trust should be accorded to the profession in exchange for an acceptance that schools are accountable to parents and society for their stewardship. The final report proposed that a broad, balanced foundation should be maintained at key stages 1 to 3, but the statutory requirements should be reduced (and be less prescriptive) at each key stage with the content of each subject divided into a statutory core and optional studies supplemented by material for use at the discretion of the teacher.

The most significant aspect of the Dearing interim and final reports, however, is their subtext which presages a more significant restructuring of the learning process in secondary education. Whereas the National Curriculum in 1988 sought to establish a broad, balanced traditional curriculum for all pupils from 5 to 16, the Dearing interim report argues for serious consideration to be given to a different approach to the post-14 age group. This is to see '14 as a distinctive staging post in the structuring of education [followed by] . . . a new approach to the education of students in the 14–18 age range [which would] specify a number of pathways which lead through in an easily intelligible and coherent way from Key Stage 4 to post 16 education and training' (Dearing 1993:25). It is a continental model where 'in the rest of Europe 16 is not a particularly significant stage in schooling and post 14 many of our neighbours place particular value on technical and vocational education. In France, Germany and the Netherlands . . . about 25% of students go to schools which specialise in some form of technical or vocational education' (p.25). The final report argues for new pathways to be developed for 14- to 16-year-olds: 'the academic pathway' and, to be worked out over the next few years, 'the vocational pathway', which maintains a broad educational component, and the possibility of 'the occupational pathway', which might consider the role of developing competence to do a job or a narrow range of jobs.

The Dearing proposals and suggestions are consistent with other policy developments and indicate a framework for restructuring which would gradually leave 5 to 14 as a general foundation of secondary education. A Circular from the new Further Education Funding Council in September 1993, announcing that colleges would be free to recruit even 13- or 14-year-old students, prompted the *Times Educational Supplement* to refer to the new 'watershed at 14 plus'. Students will be given the option not only of what they study – vocational courses as well as GCSEs – but also of where they study – college as well as school.

The Government's intention to strengthen vocational programmes has been apparent for some time. The 1991 White Paper *Education and Training for the Twenty-first Century* (DES 1991) sought to promote a vocational skill-based curriculum which would achieve parity of esteem with the academic:

Young people and adults need a clear framework of qualifications to measure their success in education and training. We need to build up a modern system of academic and vocational qualifications which are equally valued. They must both set a high standard and offer ladders of opportunity after sixteen and throughout working life . . .

Vocational qualifications in this country have been undervalued and underused. A major reform is underway to produce clear, nationally recognised qualifications. The reform is led by the National Council for Vocational Qualifications . . . the NCVQ should work with others to develop criteria for accrediting more vocational qualifications.

(DES 1991)

At the same time, a framework of principles was designed to ensure the quality of all A level and AS syllabuses. New diplomas will encompass these academic (e.g. A levels) and vocational (NVQ) qualifications. (A range of general NVQs will be developed for young people to cover broad occupational areas and enable a variety of career choices.) The Government intends that these principles should control the development of syllabuses, limiting assessment by coursework and establishing examinations at the end of courses as the norm.

The narrow focus of NVQs has been the subject of much criticism. It has been argued that the qualifications have lost touch with reality. They are tailored to specific jobs rather than setting a core standard, for example you just have to know the mathematics related to one job. This may be alright in the short term but what about a job in five years time? Similarly it has been argued that NVQs need significant amendment to be suitable for young people because they are too focused on one or two areas and have no perspective of what will be needed in ten years time: 'They will be alright for adults because they encourage people to get recognition for skills they have already acquired and this can improve morale. But it does not improve skill levels. It simply certifies levels which already exist'. The piloting of the more general GNVQ, which emphasizes cross-curricular themes and core skills, has been designed to counter criticisms of the narrowness of NVQs.

The principal thrust of Government policy is the creation of a foundation of secondary education, leaving young people to enter a system of tripartite streams from 14 to 19: an academic stream of (A levels), a technical stream (GNVQ: an advanced level general

vocational qualification) and a modern stream of practical skill
development (NVQs).

Stratifying learning into types of self-governing institutions

The 1992 White Paper celebrated 'diversity and parental choice [to]
allow schools to develop in different ways' (DFE 1992:9). Diversity offers parents and children greater choice of schools: private
and State, county and voluntary, various types of comprehensive,
grammar and bilateral, City Technology Colleges (CTCs) and grant-
maintained (GM) schools. Some schools will choose to specialize
in music or technology or in languages. Diversity, it is proposed,
extinguishes the anathema of uniformity which 'in educational
provision presupposes that all children have basically the same
educational needs. The reality is that children have different needs.
The provision of education should be geared more to local circumstances and individual needs: hence our commitment to diversity in
education' (pp.3–4).

This discussion in the White Paper implied, however, that specialization might proceed beyond different emphases of subject into
different *types* of learning and school: academic, technological and
creative. These distinctions recall the terms of tripartite education –
grammar, technical and modern – outlined in the 1938 Spens Report
and the 1943 Norwood Report, and introduced into the secondary
system after the Second World War. Indeed the 1992 White Paper
refers affectionately to this tripartite system of secondary schools
which, it implied, would have proved an ideal education system if
it had only been supported by a National Curriculum! Like the
1940s reports, the 1992 White Paper expressed its commitment to
'parity of esteem' between different types of school. It is argued that
schools could develop such specialization 'within existing powers':
'it generally does not constitute a significant change of character
requiring the approval of the Secretary of State. If schools wish to
develop in this way responding to the aspirations of parents and
local economic needs, then it is entirely appropriate that they should
use the discretion vested in them to do so' (DFE 1992).

While the 1992 White Paper celebrated diversity and alluded to
the virtues of a tripartite education system, it denied that any such
specialization or differentiation of institutions entailed selection:
'Specialisation is often confused with selection . . . a school that
specialises is not necessarily one that applies rigid academic criteria
for entry, for a non-selective school can also choose to specialise'

(p.9). Yet the word 'selection' appeared in a list of prescribed values together with 'specialisation' and 'standards'. Moreover, the White Paper acknowledged that selection *could* take place through parental choice: 'the selection that takes place is parent driven' (p.10). The emerging research evidence (DFE 1992) indicates that social selection, resisted but never eliminated by post-war social democracy, is once more being released and reinforced by the market mechanisms set in place by legislation.

Although the 1988 ERA introduced the possibility of schools 'opting out' into grant-maintained status, it is a contested issue as to whether the originating conception for GM schools saw them as the future of all schools, as a privileged sector like the old direct grant schools, or as an exception (for schools seeking to escape supposed 'undesirable' LEAs!). The norm was, arguably, intended to be locally managed schools within an LEA but accorded considerable discretion over the use of resources within local strategic policy planning. Yet, since 1991, ministers have been promoting a very different policy that GM status should become a norm not an exception. Institutional autonomy rather than discretion has now become the Government's key value: 'More diversity allows schools to respond more effectively to the needs of the local and national community. The greater their autonomy, the greater the responsiveness of schools', especially to parents who 'know best the needs of their children – certainly better than educational theorists and administrators' (DFE 1992:2).

Following the 1993 Education Act the autonomy provided by GM status supposedly becomes the key to the future quality of schools. Yet the trend towards opting out has slowed considerably. The Government fell short of its target of 1,500 GM schools by April 1994 (in October 1993 the number of GM schools stood at 693), although the Government tried to revive its flagship policy by funding three regional GM school centres in the Midlands and the North (east and west) where only 50 schools had opted out. Despite pressures on public expenditure, the Government has sought to maintain incentives for schools to opt out of their LEA by giving almost twice as much capital funding to the GM sector and by giving schools up to £1,500 to cover 'relevant expenses' where there has been a parental ballot.

The 1993 Education Act extends opting out to special schools and provides an opportunity for Christian or Muslim schools to opt into GM status. This Act will require the governing bodies of all LEA schools to consider a GM ballot once a year. The Secretary of State has taken powers both to declare a ballot void if he or she believes there has been impropriety and to limit what an LEA can spend on its publicity efforts.

Increasing State regulation

Thus the emphases of the 1992 and 1993 legislation changes mark a significant change for education. The strategies of increasing the powers of State regulation, the forces of market choice and the extent of privatization have served to erode institutions designed to support educational opportunity and local democracy. School segregation and social polarization have been a direct consequence of exposing education to unmediated market forces. Whereas in Scotland the comprehensive system had 'increased social mix, reduced the attainment gap between pupils from different backgrounds and contributed to a rising standard of attainment among pupils from all social backgrounds, the current legislation has in England quite clearly led to a widening of educational inequalities'. The Government's agenda seems to have congealed into a Platonic vision of education as a means of securing social selection and control during a period of social and economic crisis: a vision in which educational and political inequality go hand in hand.

The defining characteristic of the present restructuring by the Government of pre- and post-16 education is the attack upon the democratic foundations of local education. Its attempt to remove schools and colleges from local politics represents the termination of the post-war social democratic settlement in which local government played the pivotal role in the development of public services for all. The de-democratizing of local education is not a peripheral element, but is central to the underlying purpose of the Government's reform agenda (see Ranson 1993).

The paucity of learning in the market-place

The organizing principles of an education market are such as to render it intrinsically flawed as a means of improving learning and achievement: it can only radically contract them. Rules and relationships develop with inexorable force to erode the capacity of schools and locally elected authorities to secure educational opportunity for all. Markets, despite the rhetoric, deny opportunity for most. Supporters as well as opponents acknowledge that the logic of the market requires the creation of inequality (see Gray 1993).

Competition forces schools to see each other as rivals striving to gain the advantage that will secure survival. The emerging research evidence suggests, however, that from this rivalry emerges a hierarchy of esteem with schools increasingly inclined to select and exclude pupils so as to produce a school population likely to shine in the national league tables (see Jonathan 1989; Echols *et al.* 1990; Ball 1993). In this market hothouse only some parents acquire their 'choices': those with time, resources, knowledge and confidence to promote their children; or those with able children. Children with special needs may struggle to secure a place with schools at the apex of the hierarchy that celebrate academic distinction above other learning achievements. Some schools may seek to specialize in providing for this market niche. For policy-makers this illustrates 'choice and diversity'. Others believe this policy is covertly restoring a selective system in which access to an education is confined to some schools where the social characteristics of parents will determine the chances of admission.

Although the market (a parent rejecting one school for another) may jolt this or that school into improving its relative position in the league table, it also inescapably exacerbates perceptions of inequality. In this context, some schools will always suffer invidious comparison. That is what competition creates. It is a zero-sum game in which if there are to be winners there are sadly always going to be losers. Schools and parents are forced to play a game which can only disadvantage most of them and leave them powerless to change the rules. The power of resources are valued above the authority of reasons. A system of governance is thus created in which public policy is removed from public deliberation, choice and action: the only processes through which a community can devise a system of education that can meet the learning needs of all.

Markets, then, cannot solve the problems we face: indeed, they ensure that we stand no chance of solving them. Those problems – the restructuring of work, environmental erosion, the fragmentation of society – present issues of identity, well-being, rights, liberty, opportunity, and justice which cannot be resolved by individuals acting in isolation. Nor can they be resolved by our staging some kind of hypothetical exit, since we cannot stand outside or beyond them. Markets can only exacerbate these problems which are public in nature and confront the whole community. Deliberation, judgement and public choice are inescapable. Only the democratic processes of the public domain can enable members of a locality to articulate and reconcile the different values and needs which they believe to be central to the welfare of the communities in which they live. Given this understanding, local democracy – far from being a burden upon a community – is the only institutional setting which can provide it with the freedom and justice to flourish. As Dunn (1992:vii) argues, 'In the face of the obscure and extravagantly complicated challenges of the human future, our most urgent common need at present is to learn how to act together more effectively.' The challenge for our time is to reconstitute the conditions for a learning society in which all are empowered to develop and contribute their capacities. This will depend upon renewing the democratic foundations of the public domain and realizing – at precise points and within specific sectors – the ideal of civil society (see Gellner 1994).

In search of an alternative

Although education had, since the 1988 Education Reform Act, been subjected to the most pervasive reforms since the Second World War, by 1990 the education service became the focus of widespread criticism in speeches, papers, inquiries and leader articles expressing concern about declining standards and the exodus from education at 16+. One of the most influential voices to be raised was that of Sir Claus Moser, Warden of Wadham College, Oxford and a distinguished statistician. In his 1990 presidential address to the annual meeting of the British Association for the Advancement of Science, he warned that Britain was in danger of becoming the worst educated of all the advanced countries. In this widely reported address, and in a subsequent BBC2 television programme (*Learning to Fail*), he set out a powerful critique of the performance of British education: he was 'sad and angry that hundreds of thousands of children (indeed the majority of our children) have educational experiences not worthy of a civilized nation'.

School standards in Britain, he believed, had declined and were the worst in Europe. The root problem, he argued, is that Britain does not care as much about education as other countries do. This attitude he saw as a residue of the old Whig tradition: educate a few for leadership rather than the population as a whole. He argued that education must become a top priority and called for a new national commitment to education to be expressed in a Royal Commission on Education. This would be conducted in the context of the Government's and Parliament's failure to develop the vision needed to arrest Britain's decline. Not surprisingly, perhaps, the Government immediately turned down this call for a Royal Commission (although the National Commission on Education was set up by other means: see below).

Some months after Sir Claus Moser's speech, Prince Charles's Shakespeare Anniversary Speech continued the challenge reproducing many of the same arguments. He accused the educational establishment of failing children and depriving them of their cultural heritage: one in seven children, he said, leaves primary school 'functionally illiterate'; 40 per cent leave school with no qualifications; basic skills are weak; while only a third of 16- to 18-year-olds stay on in school. He attacked child-centred teaching, while too much vocational emphasis was leading to neglect of culture, forcing Shakespeare off the curriculum. Sanity should be restored, he proposed, before schools produce an entire generation of culturally disinherited young people. Sir Christopher Ball, Director of the Royal Society of Arts' project into post-16 education, in an important report introduced more worrying statistics (for example, that fewer than 20 per cent of pupils achieve two A levels or BTEC) and argued for a national campaign for learning: first, because 'learning pays', it is prudent for individuals and employers to invest in education and training; second, to encourage models of lifelong learning to prepare for workplace readiness; and third, to expand supply side first, in order to create a virtuous circle – increased demand for education/training produces a growth in provision and expanding provision engenders a rising demand.

If there are problems with education, a number of commentators are in no doubt about their source. Corelli Barnett writing in the *Sunday Times* in May 1991 attacked the inertia and vested interests of education. There was clearly a 'need to replace the traditional educational ethos with a training ethos that defines performance targets and emphasises cost efficiency. A fundamental cultural change is needed.' In a lecture in June 1990 Peter Morgan, Director of the Institute of Directors, blamed academics. He attacked the pernicious influence of the 'academic mould' of a 'useless' education system: the problem is academics who see the function of education to sift out an élite for a liberal education of the inner nature, consigning to the dustbin the remainder who become alienated from education while alienating the élite from business and commerce. A *Times* editorial in August 1990 similarly attacked 'educationalists' (particularly 'the social engineering ambitions fashionable amongst sociologists') who dominate attitudes towards teaching and have resisted the attempts of successive Education Secretaries to rescue educational standards.

Yet it is in the final reports of Her Majesty's Senior Chief Inspector (1990, 1991) that the achievements and failings of the service are most judiciously held in balance. Eric Bolton censured the indiscriminate attacks, finding much to applaud in teaching, including levels of achievement and increased rates of participation beyond 16. Moreover, there was no evidence that standards were falling and there were early signs of improvement following the 1988 reforms. He acknowledged, however, that nearly a third of 5- to 16-year-olds (two million children) were still receiving a limited education and that a third of all primary and secondary schools had been performing poorly (two-thirds of 9- to 11-year-olds were underachieving and reading standards were unsatisfactory in one in five schools). Long-term failings continued to confront schools, in particular poor standards of achievement amongst specific groups, especially inner-city children and the less academically able. In the more deprived parts of the education service, children learn in poorly maintained buildings and experience the poverty of resources more than others, with high proportions of them (68 per cent) leaving at 16. There is a stubborn statistic, the Senior Chief Inspector concluded, of one in three children receiving a poor education.

While any concluding analysis must, therefore, point to the need for considerable improvement in the face of daunting constraints of resource, deep-seated problems undoubtedly remain. The task is to establish a clearer identification of the problem and its cause. The Senior Chief Inspector's account provides the basis for an analysis of the entrenched pattern of disadvantage and underachievement. It is not lack of capacity or educability of the disadvantaged which explain underachievement: it is the conditions which have eroded the motivation to learn or take seriously an education that all too clearly has provided little meaning or purpose to their lives.

The continuing concern about the quality of learning and achievement in our schools has provoked a series of studies and reports which set out their analyses of the malaise facing education and their agendas for further reform of the service. We select five of these reform programmes to illustrate the different interpretations of change to improve teaching and learning:

- the tripartist agenda
- the educational professional agenda
- the institutional diversity and choice agenda
- the Labour Party agenda
- the National Commission on Education agenda.

We shall argue that each of these agendas, while offering important contributions, fails to address the predicament facing schools or to provide an analysis which meets the challenge of regenerating the quality of learning in a period of social change.

The reform agenda of the tripartist tradition

Responding to Sir Claus Moser's critique of the education service, Channel Four invited five leading academics to 'investigate the state of our education'. The report (Channel Four Commission on Education: *Every Child in Britain* (1991), which was led by Professor Alan Smithers) attributes the poor performance of the post-war British economy, and the inadequate levels of educational attainment in Britain compared with the rest of Europe, to an educational system dominated by narrowly academic grammar schools.

> The decline of technical schools is one of the tragedies of British education. It seems highly probable that there is a link between Britain's post war economic performance and the withering away of such schools and their replacement by the narrowly academic and less vocational grammar schools.
>
> (p.11)

The report argued that the comprehensive reforms of the 1960s merely presented a watered-down version of the grammar school curriculum and may have actually increased inequality by removing the 'escape route to grammar schools for those working class youngsters lucky enough to gain entry' (p.11). The needs of the majority of young people have been neglected, causing them to feel discarded, to underachieve or to drop out of education. The dominance of the academic tradition in the system has frustrated many attempts to provide a more practical/technical education for the majority. Even when technology is introduced into the curriculum it 'is less about actually *making* things, than about talking and writing about making them' (p.14).

The Channel Four commissioners concluded their report by proposing four 'policy principles':

- . . . a system of schooling based on pupils' attainments and career ambitions.
- To make learning more attractive, the curriculum for pupils from about the age of 14 must be made more relevant to their likely activities after compulsory schooling. This will involve clearer choices between distinct pathways.
- For teaching to become more effective (and more attractive to teachers), we must make the task of the teacher easier. This involves ensuring that pupils in each class are of much more even attainments than at present.
- Schooling attainments must be made more easily understood

by parents, pupils and employers . . . (and) examinations
must be rigorous at all levels of attainment. The result of
externally-marked tests should be reported separately from
course-work assessed by the pupil's own teacher. School-
leaving qualifications should be based on *average* attainments
in a broad and balanced groups of subjects.

(p.25)

Learning would, in the view of the commissioners, be better
organized around attainment, with progress from one year to the
next being related to levels of attainment rather than just to the
chronological age of pupils. Learning, they argued, would also be
facilitated if pupils were grouped for the purposes of teaching within
similar bands of attainment:

With a narrower spread of pupil attainments, it will become
easier for the teacher to spend a greater proportion of each
school-period teaching the class as a whole; rather than
breaking each class into groups working at different levels.
This should make it easier to maintain systematic teaching.
We also recommend that teachers modify their teaching styles
to promote a more ordered teaching environment as observed
in continental schools.

(p.28)

Following a common (more basic) national curriculum in the first
three years of secondary education, pupils would, at 14, choose
between three pathways: academic, technical and vocational. The
academic pathway would lead to a grouped diploma, based on a
core of English, mathematics, science and a foreign language, and
would be a rigorous preparation for A levels. The technical pathway 'would seek to develop talents for making things, designing
things and being good with people' (p.29). This pathway would be
based on the same academic core, but with options for practical
courses. It would prepare pupils for more technological A levels or
their equivalents. Pupils in this pathway would be expected to proceed to higher education at the appropriate level. The vocational
pathway would be similar to the technical one but 'involve greater
specialisation in the work the young people might move into'
and would 'take place in a combination of educational and work
settings' (p.29). Some youngsters could enter employment before
16 as long as they were able to attend approved training courses
including a day-release at college. The commissioners emphasize
that there would be opportunities for young people to move

between pathways, 'though switching might involve taking longer to reach certain qualifications' (p.29).

The reform agenda of the educational profession tradition

As the 1992 election approached, 14 professors of education and allied disciplines wrote to the *Guardian* declaring:

> a modern society cannot prosper with a narrow education base and socially divisive hierarchies of schools. High quality education is an essential investment in the skills and knowledge needed to cope with the challenges of the next century. It must not be reserved for some children in some of our schools.

They believed that education could not flourish 'as a commodity to be "traded" in the market place'. Following the publication of the Government's 1992 White Paper (*Diversity and Choice*), they joined together under the aegis of the Institute for Public Policy Research (IPPR) to publish, in 1993, their own alternative White Paper: *Education: A Different Vision* (IPPR 1993). Their analysis of the economic and social changes clarified the kind of qualities young people would need in the future. In addition to fundamental competencies in literacy and numeracy, young adults would, they argued, 'need a broader education to give them a firm grounding for the variety of work and social experiences they are likely to encounter'; in particular they would require 'imagination', 'flexibility', 'determination', and a 'sense of responsibility' (p.9). Citizens of the twenty-first century, aware of their obligations as well as their rights, will need to be vastly more proficient in many aspects of their lives than has been the case hitherto. The learning process should promote co-operation as well as individual initiative and entrepreneurship: 'the ability to live and work co-operatively with fellow adults and children will be an important element of life in the 21st century, if the social disasters of the 20th century are to be avoided' (p.18). An education system that aspires to provide opportunities equally for *all* children must support the public good of fairness, respect and freedom and must 'reject competition as the sole motivating force in education' (p.18).

The curriculum, they argue, should develop understanding as well as knowledge and skills, and should encourage positive attitudes to what young people are learning. At the primary level the curriculum should be organized around five domains of learning: literacy, numeracy, the arts, the world around us, and how the world works. The early years of secondary school should form a bridge with the primary years and lead towards a phase, from 14 to 16, which emphasizes choices within seven fields of study; modern languages are encouraged. From 16 to 18 a broader range of study should be encouraged – perhaps even 'a five A level slate' – and there should be much less division between the academic and the vocational: 'Whether students embark on what are usually called the "vocational" or the "academic" track, they should be able to acquire both "pure" and "applied" knowledge, understanding and skills, and there should be parity of esteem for what they achieve' (p.53).

Learning, the report insists, is not a commodity to be bought or sold, but a 'transaction' or a 'conversation' between teacher and learner. The authorities in this conversation are 'those who, from within an educational tradition so disparaged by the Government, are called upon to initiate the next generation into the achievements of literature and of history and into the wonders of scientific enquiry, as well as encouraging them to play their own part in that continuing process' (p.16). It is the leading role of the teacher to introduce the next generation to culture and to the critical tools which they will need. 'Teachers are among the most important members of society' (p.11) and their expertise and support will be the key to an effective education of all citizens. Whatever the framework of education 'it will always be the teachers who actually create the quality' (p.72). Because the professionalism which underpins this quality has been threatened by the increasing centralization of power, the time has now come 'to give the teaching profession a large measure of responsibility for its own regulation and development' (p.73) through the creation of a General Teaching Council.

The professors argue that if the learning needs of young people are to be supported, the institutions of accountable governance, so eroded in recent years, need to be restored. Realizing democratic educational values will require a common vision: 'a vision which transcends but accommodates diversity of outlook and which is constructed out of painstaking dialogue, rather than imposed from above' (p.22). This will require structures that will enable sharing of power between education partners at all levels. Their conception of power-sharing would require central and local government 'to share power with those groups in society that have a legitimate interest in the aims and processes of education in our schools' (p.23). Genuine debate and consultation between democratically elected local and national representatives and education interest groups can, they believe, no longer be trusted to the adversarial system of party politics operating in central and local government. Power needs to be shared in a fair and just manner, so as to allow all the interested parties to debate, for example, the National Curriculum: 'Any redistribution of those powers would require a new act of Parliament to establish policy making structures that guarantee the entitlement of different interest groups to participate in debate about the form and content of the National Curriculum' (p.20).

Parents have a significant part to play, but not in the role cast for them by the present Government as 'inquisitor, complainant and vigilante' (p.41). It is acknowledged that if standards of learning are to be improved then 'parents will need closer involvement with schooling' (p.42), but in a different role: they 'should see themselves as joint producers of education with teachers and should work in genuine partnership' (p.41). The professors propose that 'if parental participation and partnership are to be a reality for all parents, formal participation at the class and school level, set within a legislative framework, is essential' (p.43). They propose, therefore, that home–school associations, funded by a government grant, should be set up in each school and incorporate all parents as members. These associations would not preoccupy themselves, as so often at present, with fund-raising, but become 'a forum for passing over knowledge and information about formal schooling to parents, and the passing of information on home learning to teachers' (p.43).

The associations would include 'class associations' as the principal method of bringing teachers and parents together to 'discuss matters relating to children's learning, progress and achievement, curriculum, assessment, recording, teaching methods, behaviour in schools and school organisation' (p.43). Parents would work with teachers to encourage other parents who have been rather reluctant to visit the school to become more involved. The associations would encourage home–school liaison by organizing publications and communication, co-ordinating home–school learning schemes and homework arrangements. 'Written home–school parents' educational agreements (contracts) for every pupil would be developed within the framework of a home–school association' (p.44). The associations would liaise with but not replace governing bodies, and they would be consulted at local level 'when important decisions were being made on education' (p.44). Similarly, at national level their representatives would be consulted.

The professors conclude that they have 'tried to develop a vision of the future that recognises the likelihood of lifelong learning, the need for a highly skilled, knowledgeable and well-informed citizenry in the 21st century, imaginative, flexible and willing to retrain in childhood, adulthood and through and beyond the Third Age of healthy retirement' (p.78).

Reforming the tradition of diversity and choice

David Hargreaves's report, *The Mosaic of Learning* (1994) belongs to a tradition close to the Government's own agenda. Although published by Demos, an independent think tank broadly on the left of British politics, it endorses many of the items on the Government's reform agenda, particularly in respect of parental choice, initial teacher education and school management.

Hargreaves's report is structured around what he calls five 'seeds' of change:

Seed 1: Increase in diversity of school provision and parental choice   The conventional comprehensive school has outlived its usefulness and should be replaced by schools which are highly differentiated and specialized by curriculum area (for example, science and technology, languages, the arts) or by belief (for example, religious schools: Christian, Muslim, Jewish). The comprehensive principle is retained: 'it is perfectly possible to have specialised schools where admission is not based on some general ability'. Nor, given the requirements of the National Curriculum, would there be any danger of such schools sacrificing breadth to depth. Hargreaves's' argument is that, since 'many adolescents are less enthusiastic about school than about education', some form of specialization might well increase motivation and achievement (p.20).

Seed 2: Better-organized schools and new types of teacher   Schools should be managed by a professional manager. A smaller number of full-time better-trained, highly paid professional teachers should be supported by a range of assistant teachers: 'A hospital run entirely by doctors without the support of nurses would be grossly wasteful. Why do we not see schools without assistants to teachers as similarly prodigal with scarce resources?' (p.24). Both heads and teachers should be on five-year contracts which should be renewed only when their competence has been confirmed: 'Those who for whatever reason contribute less should with reason forfeit some pay and those who become seriously deficient cannot expect to have their appointments renewed' (pp.24–5). Schools should contract out substantial parts of their teaching functions to a range of outside agencies so that secondary pupils spend less of their time in school, where many become bored and therefore troublesome. The boundaries around school should become highly permeable, with students and a whole range of other adults moving back and forth. The best way to create deviant youth cultures, maintains Hargreaves, is to segregate them by age in institutions many do not like.

Seed 3: The establishment of civic education   'The notion of non-denominational core RE to be offered in all schools as a buttress to moral education is becoming less and less viable and should now be abandoned' (p.34). A core civic education could be taught more readily and, argues Hargreaves, 'with more conviction by most teachers' (p.39). All schools should offer a common civic component designed for a society that, although pluralist, requires some basic shared values to ensure national cohesion. Hargreaves sees this as an urgent requirement: 'If over the next few years the schools cannot respond with a rapid improvement in civic and moral education, then more authoritarian solutions to law and order problems will be adopted by politicians' (p.40).

Seed 4: The advance of the new technologies   Schools should invest further in the new technologies, which are becoming cheaper and more attractive as they open up new possibilities for teaching and learning. Computer games, argues Hargreaves, 'do not lower their expectations because of the perceived background of the player'. They motivate and challenge: 'If the game is hard, the machine frustrates, but is far less likely than a teacher to humiliate' (p.41). Moreover, the new technologies provide students with the opportunity of working more at home while keeping in touch with teachers and fellow learners via the technology. 'Schools are still modelled on a curious mix of the factory, the asylum and the prison' (p.43). An increased investment in the new technologies could ensure that 'the school feels less like a school – a sensation that is profoundly refreshing' (pp.43–4).

Seed 5: Better research to guide education policy and practice   There are no equivalents in education to medicine, where new drugs or treatments are subjected to clinical trial and testing. At present the selection of courses and teaching methods depends upon subjective judgements or the preferences of teachers rather than upon research evidence: 'Very little of the implementation of educational innovation, especially in the curriculum and methods of teaching and learning, is preceded by a period of rigorous trial and test' (p.44). Educational research, argues Hargreaves, should be concentrated into a small number of research institutes working in conjunction with innovative schools with a view to providing better guidance on educational policy and practice: 'we need less educational research but of a very much higher average quality' (p.51).

Hargreaves concludes by stating that 'schools for the next century' should:

- be smaller, differentiated and specialised, giving more choice to students, parents and teachers
- be independent institutions, financed on the basis of a national formula, accountable to parents and collaborating in consortia as voluntary associations
- be committed, within a national strategy for school improvement, to quality assurance and 'total quality' schemes in place of traditional school inspection
- be staffed and managed in new ways by a wider range of personnel and by a richer variety of teachers
- have a head teacher as leading professional but with a professional manager in charge of administration
- have a core of full-time, highly trained professional teachers, on five-year renewable contracts, supported by a range of assistant teachers and part-time teachers who also work in other fields
- contract out substantial parts of their teaching functions, so that secondary pupils spend less of their time in school
- be permeable to their community, to business and the world of working adults, so that the boundaries between school and the outside world weaken
- be committed to a common civic education for a cohesive but pluralistic society, but with more religious schools for those who prefer them
- be better equipped with the new interactive technologies
- be guided in their policies and practice by substantially better research conducted by selected research centres in close association with schools.

(pp.53–4)

Reforming the tradition of open access and widening opportunities

The Labour Party's policy statement on education – *Opening Doors to a Learning Society* (1994) – was issued shortly after Tony Blair took up the leadership of the Labour Party. It offers the 'vision of an educated democracy in which good education ceases to be restricted as a competitive prize at arbitrary points throughout life but becomes the very basis for economic, political and cultural success' (p.3). It

argues for 'a new constitutional settlement for our education services: one that enshrines the principles of access for all, quality and
equity, continuity, accountability, and partnership' (p.31).

It proposes five key 'principles for education policy making':

> *Access for all*: Education should be about opening doors and keep-
> ing them open as wide as possible for as long as possible . . .
> *Quality and equity*: . . . Our current system is based on low ex-
> pectations and the assumptions that the vast majority lack ability.
> Labour believes that quality education demands a comprehens-
> ive provision for all stages, and rejects any system in which a
> few are selected at the expense of the vast majority.
> *Continuity*: Labour believes we need a system of education that
> extends horizons, increases expectations and enhances the
> aspirations of each person. Education is a life-long process and
> it should not be terminated at arbitrary points . . .
> *Accountability*: Education services belong to the whole commun-
> ity, and until recently it had always been accepted that they
> were accountable to the whole community . . . Everyone must
> feel they have a stake in the system . . .
> *Partnership*: . . . Central government should create the frame-
> work for education whilst the local delivery of services must
> be the responsibility of those who are democratically and pro-
> fessionally accountable . . . Confrontation must be replaced by
> co-operation.
>
> (pp.4–5)

The document highlights the need for nursery education with
an undertaking 'to ensure that all 3 and 4 year-olds whose parents
want it have access to quality nursery education, co-ordinated with
quality childcare provision on a flexible basis to meet children's
needs and parents' circumstances' (p.6). It emphasizes that the
prevailing pattern of provision 'is diverse, of variable quality and
involves statutory, voluntary, and private agencies' (p.8). It calls for
comprehensive provision and for increased co-ordination between
the voluntary and statutory sectors. It promises 'a curriculum entitlement for 3 and 4 year old children which will concentrate on
language development as a priority' and pledges Labour 'to give
particular encouragement to promoting parental involvement in
early years education' (p.6).

While supporting the need for a national curriculum, the statement opposes the current version and states that 'Labour will further the process of replacing the prescriptive national syllabus with

a framework national curriculum . . . which values local flexibility and the professional discretion of teachers' (p.15). Labour would also replace the current national testing arrangements with 'assessment procedures that have the confidence of parents and teachers alike' (p.16). It would aim for 'genuine parity of esteem between the academic and the vocational' through the introduction of 'a unified qualification structure that will incorporate the best practice from existing qualifications, whether academically oriented or geared to vocational skills' (p.23). A General Certificate of Further Education (GCFE) would be created for the majority for whom the A/AS level is inappropriate. The GCFE would build upon the strengths and experiences of the present GCSE and both these qualifications would be integrated as part of a continuous structure for the 14 to 19+ age group. All GCFE courses would contain core elements 'to ensure that a balance was maintained between academic and vocational courses and between classroom contact and the world of work' (p.24).

The policy statement emphasizes the need for schools to develop 'strong corporate identities founded on and supported by co-operative and purposeful leadership'. Successful schools, it argues, are characterized by 'a positive and disciplined environment conducive to learning, which in turn requires high quality, well-trained, and confident teachers, operating in safe, well maintained buildings, with appropriate class sizes'. It sees motivation as 'the single most important factor in education' (p.10). Students become motivated by acquiring self-discipline within a context that is both orderly and well structured. Parental support is critical in creating such contexts: schools must help pupils and parents 'understand how important it is that parents support children in learning at home and view home as part of their children's learning environment'. For parents to fulfil a more active role in the education of their children their collective voice needs to be heard 'on such matters as children's learning, progress and achievement, matters related to curriculum, assessment, recording, teacher methods, behaviour in schools, and school organisation'. A Labour government would encourage the development of home/school associations and 'ensure that written home/school contracts are developed for every pupil within the framework of the home/school association' (p.11).

Synthesizing the traditions

The National Commission on Education's reform agenda – *Learning to Succeed* (1993a) was the report ensuing from its foundation in

July 1991, following Sir Claus Moser's 1990 intervention. Although his call for a Royal Commission had been turned down by the Government, it generated much support both within and outside the world of education. The British Association decided, therefore, to set up its own independent inquiry, with the support of the Royal Society, the British Academy and the Fellowship (later the Royal Academy) of Engineering. The Paul Hamlyn Foundation funded the work of the commission, which in addition to its report has produced two volumes of supporting papers (NCE 1993b, 1994).

The most serious shortcoming of education in the UK, the commission argues, 'is its failure to enable not just a minority but a large majority of young people to obtain as much from their education as they are capable of achieving' (NCE 1993a). While a minority of academically able young people receive a good, if narrow education supported by appropriate and efficiently run provision, the education received by the majority is of 'more variable benefit' (NCE 1993a). Their talents are neither valued nor developed enough and many leave school with disturbingly poor levels of basic literacy and numeracy.

The serious mistake in the development of education throughout the century has been to model an education for the majority on that prepared for an élite, that is, a liberal, academic, education. 'Attempts to move the emphasis of provision at least some distance from the notion of a liberal education rooted in the past towards the needs of industry and the demands of work in the future have repeatedly been frustrated' (p.30). Education over the past 30 years has been 'thoroughly inadequate for a leading industrial nation in the last quarter of the twentieth century' (p.25).

The commission's 'vision for the future' emphasizes that the key to the country's survival will depend upon its capacity to enhance the knowledge and skills of its people, to keep pace with scientific and technological advance, to compete in a global economy and to keep up with the general pace of social and cultural change. Because the key to success will be the capacity to apply the knowledge, the commission emphasizes the significance of 'applied intelligence' which can turn ideas into practice. It warns that the accelerating pace of the 'scientific revolution' could present a threat to social cohesion if some are denied opportunities to become 'knowledge workers'. It insists that education and training provision should be developed to suit the needs and capabilities of the whole population.

While education must be developed to underpin the economic success that is necessary to improve the quality of life of everybody, the commission also reinforces the significance of 'the wider purposes of education'. Its vision statement reflects this concern for personal and social well-being within a rapidly changing world:

1 In all countries *knowledge and applied intelligence* have become central to economic success and personal and social well-being.
2 In the United Kingdom much higher achievement in education and training is needed to match world standards.
3 Everyone must want to learn and have ample opportunity and encouragement to do so.
4 All children must achieve a good grasp of literacy and basic skills early on as the foundation for learning throughout life.
5 The full range of people's abilities must be recognised and their development rewarded.
6 High-quality learning depends above all on the knowledge, skill effort and example of teachers and trainers.
7 It is the role of education *both* to interpret *and* pass on the values of society and to stimulate people to think for themselves and to change the world around them.

(NCE 1993a:xv)

The commission translates this vision into particular areas for action. Prime among these is teacher professionalism. The commission quotes Eric Bolton (1992) as saying that 'the most crucial factor at the heart of high quality learning is high quality teaching'. It suggests 'a way forward' that involves:

• a spiral of raised standards of entrants to teaching and the promotion of a high status profession;
• an entitlement for every teacher to rigorous training and development throughout his or her career;
• new arrangement for the pay, career progression and working conditions of teachers to establish and maintain a flourishing profession;
• a strengthening of the primary role of the teacher as an educator, in command of a range of expertise and with appropriate technological back-ups;
• coherent leadership throughout the profession, including self-regulation;
• equality of opportunity for all staff.

(p.233)

A further area for action is that of continuity: 'learning throughout life'. The report argues strongly for high quality nursery education for all 3- to 4-year-olds and for a renewed emphasis on the early years of primary schooling. It also argues for a radical overhaul of qualifications at 16 and 18. It puts forward a proposal for a modular General Education Diploma (GED). This would be awarded at two levels – Ordinary level, normally reached at 16; and Advanced level, normally at 18 – and would replace the range of qualifications, including GCSE, A levels, BTEC and both general and more specific vocational qualifications, currently available or being developed for 16- to 18-year-olds. Comprising a variety of separately certificated modules, it would offer choice and flexibility and would require greater breadth than the A level system allows.

The commission expressed concern regarding schools in disadvantaged areas. It argues for extra funding to be targeted at attracting excellent teachers to such areas. It suggests that 'appropriate salary rewards for good teachers in deprived areas are important', but also that 'professional development is vital as a source of new ideas for dealing with problems as well as a way of renewing commitment and enthusiasm for a demanding task'. It emphasizes the importance of initial teacher training, while putting forward specific proposals regarding the need for the continuing professional development of teachers: 'There should be opportunities to spend time away from school on secondment or sabbatical. Professional development vouchers might be a worthwhile option' (p.178).

The limits of the alternative agendas

There are clearly manifest differences in these five alternative agendas: for example, the divergent perspectives on how best to support teachers and to ensure that teaching develops as a profession; the issues around school organization, pupil grouping and differentiated learning; and the various proposals relating to assessment and recording procedures at the key transition points of 5, 11, 14 and 16. There is also much of importance in the agendas: the insistence on teaching as an extremely demanding professional occupation; the need for teachers to entertain high, though realistic, expectations of all students; the acknowledgement that schools matter and can make a difference; the emphasis on education as lifelong; and the importance of support and restructuring in the early years and at the 16+ transition point. Yet we argue that they also share a number of limitations which cause them to fail to address fully the needs of education reform in our time.

Their failure to grasp the magnitude of disadvantage

In all the agendas we have reviewed there is a yawning gap where we would expect to find a serious and considered analysis of the nature of disadvantage in contemporary society and, crucially, its impact on learning and on the formal mechanisms of schooling. Several of the reports have a notion of certain schools serving disadvantaged areas, but the experience of living and learning in such areas is taken for granted rather than explored. The assumption is that we know everything we need to know about disadvantage; the problem is defined, not in terms of the nature of disadvantage itself, but in terms of the need to realize that disadvantage can be overcome. There even seems to be a sense of embarrassment about disadvantage, as if it is a concept too closely associated with deficit modes of thinking that have no place in upbeat alternative agendas for the new millennium. The failure here is to imagine that the will to overcome disadvantage has any substance without a commitment to understanding what exactly disadvantage is within contemporary society. There is a need, which none of these alternative agendas addresses, to learn about disadvantage.

Their failure to understand the social, moral and political significance of change

There is also a failure in these reports to understand structural change other than in its implications for the labour market. Change is thereby denied its social, moral and political content. There is no attempt, for example, to explore the environmental implications of change or its impact on the family and home; no attempt to understand the complex ways in which change affects relations between the private and public domains; no analysis of the uneven experience of change and the increasing dependence of large sections of society on the informal economy. Again, the assumption is that we already know about change: the task is defined in terms of the need to refocus the work of schools so as to adjust to what we know about the changing circumstances of the labour market. Any such adjustment, however, is likely to be mere tinkering unless it is accompanied by an acknowledgement that change is ubiquitous, persistent and increasingly complex in its impact on human lives. There is an urgent need to learn about historic change.

Their failure to develop a theory of learning

The failure of these agendas to grasp either the magnitude of disadvantage or the complexity of structural change leads them to an overpreoccupation with the instrumental and economic dimensions of learning at the expense of the intrinsic and moral dimensions. There is much discussion within these reports on student expectations and aspirations, on school discipline and the need for student self-discipline, on values and ethos. But these themes are invariably rationalized in terms of other ends and purposes; the moral dimension, in so far as it exists, is thereby rendered instrumental and extrinsic. What is missing is any sense of how learning must be reconceived in terms of the crushing effect of structural transformations that fragment and radically disrupt human experience. There is a need to develop a theory of learning that meets the challenge of these transformations.

Their failure to develop a new vision

In short, we see the need for a deeper analysis of the causes and consequences of underachievement (which, we would argue, lie in the organizing assumptions of a social order that favours passivity rather than agency) and for a vision of learning which matches the challenge of the transformations of our time. The agendas offer solutions, but to problems which (as currently formulated) seem increasingly irrelevant. The problems themselves require radical reformulation through an analysis that relates them to structural change and to new forms of social and economic disadvantage. Without such an analysis the proffered solutions are likely to be little more than ameliorative: a response to symptoms, rather than a serious attempt to tackle the underlying causes. There is a need to learn new ways of thinking to match the new kinds of problems that we face.

The challenge of our time

The central challenge of our time is to transform the way people think of themselves and what they are capable of. It is only by changing the sense students have of themselves as learners that they can begin to develop their capacities and realize their potential. This purpose can only be realized if those deep-seated forces of disadvantage and discrimination, which diminish the self-esteem of learners, are addressed. Behind these forces and reinforcing them are historic changes that are altering what it is to be a person as we move towards the year 2000.

Multiple inequalities

The impact of multiple inequalities on contexts of disadvantage has been highlighted by two recent reports: the *Report of the Commission on Social Justice* (CSJ 1994) and the *Joseph Rowntree Foundation Inquiry into Income and Wealth* (JRF 1995). Both reports show that the problems associated with inequality are becoming concentrated on particular groups and areas. The poor have become poorer:

> between 1979 and 1991/2, the poorest 10 per cent saw their real incomes *fall* by 17 per cent, from £74 to £61 a week. Despite the recession, the very highest paid people in London and the South-East increased their earnings by an average of £22,000 a year between 1989 and 1991, while the bottom 50 per cent of earners took an average pay *cut* of more than £200 a year.
>
> (CSJ 1994:29–30)

This concentration of poverty on particular groups and areas has intensified their social problems, producing higher rates of family breakup, larger numbers of lone parents surviving on the margins of society, more children 'at risk', higher rates of youth unemployment, and increased levels of crime and vandalism (JRF 1995:35). 'People living on the poorest council estates are four times more likely to be a victim of crime than people living in affluent suburbs' (CSJ 1994:50).

Both reports also point to the growing polarization between 'work-rich' and 'work-poor' families: 'The changes in men's and women's employment are combining to produce a new problem – a widening gap between "work-rich" families, with one and a half or two jobs, and "work-poor" families, with no job at all . . . A woman married to an employed man is almost three times as likely to be in a job herself as a woman married to a man without a job' (p.38). The pressure on 'work-poor' families is increasing as the concentration of joblessness affects the same people for longer periods: 'The single biggest risk factor in determining whether or not a man will be unemployed this year is not his education, his previous occupation or where he lives, but whether or not he was unemployed in the last year' (p.36). These trends can in part be explained in terms of the feminization of the workforce, but again the overall picture is one of inequality with 46 per cent of employed working women working part-time, 'most of them in low-paid jobs with few pension rights and little prospect of training or promotion' (p.38). In short, 'The chances of getting into work have fallen for both men and women who are not working and whose partners are not working either' (JRF 1995:23).

The concentration of poverty and unemployment on particular groups and areas is particularly troubling given their adverse effect on the health of the unemployed and their families. For example:

> a baby whose father is an unskilled manual worker is one-and-a-half times more likely to die before the age of one as the baby of a manager or professional employee, (while) the poorest children are twice as likely as those from social class 1 to die from respiratory illness, more than four times as likely to be killed in a traffic accident . . . and more than six times as likely to die in a house fire.
>
> (CSJ 1994:43)

Unemployment compounds the health risks associated with poverty, so that 'a middle-aged man made redundant or taking early retirement is twice as likely to die within five years as a man who stays in work' (p.45). The impact of these multiple inequalities is experienced with particular intensity in certain localities: 'In Sheffield and Glasgow, people living in the most affluent areas can expect to live eight years longer than those in the most deprived areas' (p.44). In some localities deprivation is compounded by prejudice and discrimination.

Prejudice and discrimination

The Rampton (1981), Swann (1985) and Eggleston, Dunn and Anjali (1986) Reports all acknowledged the serious effect which prejudice has upon the performance of children in school, as reflected by the *Report of the Commission on Social Justice*:

> There are social processes in both schools and society at large that counter the efforts of black young people. In schools, both at and below sixth form level, we found evidence that ethnic minority pupils may be placed on courses and entered for examinations at levels significantly below those appropriate for their abilities and ambitions. Within the hidden curriculum of some schools lurk lower expectations by teachers for their

black pupils. Teachers may be unwilling to acknowledge the existence of these processes, or even redress them where they are aware of them. And black adolescents currently demonstrate the self-fulfilling prophesy by reacting to manners, speech and behaviour that appear to justify the differential expectations that surround them . . . Beyond school, the effects of racial discrimination upon employment prospects were severe. Even when young black people did attain appropriate qualifications they did not obtain jobs in equal proportions to whites either before or after participating in the Youth Opportunities or similar schemes.

(CSJ 1994:44)

Beliefs about the damaging influence of racial prejudice on learning have been expressed clearly in a North London LEA:

racism causes underachievement. It is the single most important factor, and is perceived as the most important factor by parents. Racism in schools stifles learning because children spend all their time looking for it and trying to cope with it. They are not able to be themselves and struggle to survive. Racism must be challenged and discussed constantly as part of the learning process.

Black teachers as well as black pupils are expected to fail. There is a lack of recognition. They are not seen as capable. This is how racism affects black people.

Minorities are most concerned about institutionalized racism, which occurs when the stereotyped beliefs and attitudes about ethnic minorities enter into the routines and structures of an organization. 'When curriculum planning reinforces Asian boys to do maths and science, Cypriot girls to do home economics, and Afro-Caribbean children to do RE or athletics, prejudice has been routinized'.

The Commission on Social Justice emphasizes that racial discrimination remains 'a significant element in economic, social and political injustice in the United Kingdom today' (CSJ 1994:51). Prejudice and discrimination are experienced in countless forms by the black and ethnic minorities, including racial abuse of African-Caribbean young people as well as violent attacks on Asian families. Ethnic minorities, with the exception of Chinese and African-Asian communities, are more likely to be unemployed. 'While about half of all male employees are in manual work, for Caribbeans, Pakistanis and Bangladeshis the proportion is two-thirds or more, with

Bangladeshis grossly over-represented in semi-skilled and unskilled manual work' (p.52). Although black children are more likely than white to stay on at school, their educational attainment remains often much lower than for their age group. 'Afro-Caribbean pupils are not only more likely to be excluded for bad behaviour from schools in England and Wales, but are also far less likely to go to university' (p.51).

When disadvantage and discrimination are considered together there is a danger that we are witnessing the emergence of a new minority – an underclass – who are at the receiving end of increasing multiple inequalities. What is at stake is the quality of life and the protection of basic entitlements: 'the position of the underclass', as Dahrendorf (1994:5) has argued 'is one beyond the threshold of basic opportunities of access'. Such anxieties are accentuated by consideration of the wider structural transformations now unfolding.

Structural transformations

Society is experiencing a phase of deep transition (Ranson 1994). Change is now ubiquitous, persistent and non-linear: this is the chronic condition in which we live, making for a world that is increasingly complex with the unpredictable becoming a normal part of experience. The very language now being created to characterize this transformation – 'post-modern', 'post-industrial', 'post-Fordist' – suggests the historically unprecedented complexity of our epoch in terms of what it supersedes. Such structural change and uncertainty has provoked questions that further disturb the social and political cohesion of the post-war order.

By making some members of society 'surplus to capacity', economic change brings into question one of the bases of post-war citizenship: the right to work. The issues raised are quite fundamental. What will be the nature of work in the future and who will be required to work? Do individuals need to work to express their identities, develop their capacities, acquire status and contribute as citizens to the commonwealth of the community in which they live? Will those who remain outside work be regarded as members, as citizens, by others in the community? Will they be accorded equal rights and status and power in the community?

The trends towards differentiation that characterize post-modern society creates space for innovation and change yet also threatens to undermine the very possibility of 'society'. Social fragmentation threatens the co-operation and trust that both define a community and create the possibility of collective action without which no society can survive. The most serious collective action problem is the predatory exploitation of the environment with its dramatic consequences for the quality of life and even survival. Mounting litter, traffic congestion and the prospect of global warming reveal the unintended collective consequences of our individual choices: self-interest can be self-defeating. The seductive, yet ultimately irrational compulsion of some to 'free-ride' presents perhaps the most significant challenge for future society. Parfit (1984) succinctly describes the dilemma: 'it can be better for each if he adds to pollution, uses more energy, jumps queues and breaks agreements; but if all do these things, that can be worse off for each than if none do. It is very often true, that if each rather than none does what will be better for himself, this will be worse off for everyone.' The question arises whether our society any longer possesses the social conditions to resolve the collective action problems which face it.

The economic, social and political transformations of our time are altering fundamentally the structure of experience: the capacities each person needs to flourish, what it is to live in society, the nature of work and the form taken by polity. The changes raise deep questions for the government of education and for the polity in general, concerning what is it to be a person? Is a person a passive being or possessed of powers that define his or her essential agency? Is there any such thing as a society and what is it? An aggregation of individuals or some form of social and linguistic community? What should be the nature of the polity? What is it to be a member and with what rights and duties? What distribution of power and wealth is consistent with justice and freedom? Who should take decisions and how? What forms of accountability and representation define our democracy?

Any effective response to these questions will require a capacity for renewal, for learning, from the institutions of our society as much as from each individual confronting the changed circumstances in private life. From either perspective, the problems of the time are public and require public solutions. Yet it is the public institutions which are being eroded.

There is an urgent need for fundamental change, to create a common purpose and the conditions for individuals and their communities to flourish by empowering their sense of agency and responsibility for the future. The realization of such aims depends upon the creation of a new moral and political order, both to support the development of individual powers and to create an open, public culture responsive to change. The defining quality of such an order, and the key to change, is a society which has learning as its organizing principle. There is a need for reforms that will rescue us from the mistakes of the past and prepare us more adequately for the future. Our priority must be both to change the purposes of education and to embody in the reform of social and political institutions the organizing principle of learning; and for that we need to theorize both the nature of learning and the institutional and cultural factors that shape it.

TWO

Towards a theory of learning

What the purpose of learning should be, how it should be arranged and what conditions best support its effective development have varied considerably since the Second World War. For periods there has appeared to be a consensus across society about the purposes and organization of education, but at others, and especially more recently, there have been fundamental disagreements about what learning is for and what secures achievement. The keen interest which governments have taken in the service reflects their understanding of the significance of education for the social order as well as economic development. What young people learn shapes their understanding of themselves, their capacities, and the way they will relate to others. To shape education is to seek to shape how a generation grows up and to control the distribution of the goods which flow from the structuring of capacities.

In this chapter we explore the very different conceptions of learning which have prevailed in the post-war period and what they imply for developing the sense of worth and capacity for young people. Having discussed the structures which underlay these different patterns of learning we seek to develop an analytical model of learning which will enable us to shape the discussion of how schools in contexts of disadvantage approach learning and teaching.

Changing conceptions of learning

Learning can pursue diverse purposes which do not always sit easily together. The rigorous pursuit of one set of purposes may impede the accomplishment of others. An insistent preoccupation with the economic function of education, seeking to prepare young people with the skills and attitudes that will be required by their future employers, will probably divert schools from the purpose of meeting the personal development needs of each young person. Music and art may, under one set of priorities, have to give way to learning about business and technology. Furthermore, a concern to promote the culture of the past may conflict with objectives held by the polity to reform and modernize society.

The dilemmas posed for society by such diverse educational purposes have been resolved by emphasis and choice. These choices typically reflect deep underlying values about the function of education and the form of society and polity it might help to create. The controversies surrounding the form of education desired by a society involve an argument about the priority which should be given to particular values. The shaping of education is the shaping of generation and society. The most articulate expression of these relationships has been provided by Williams (1965:145–6):

> The business of organising education – creating types of institution, deciding lengths of courses, agreeing conditions of entry and duration – is certainly important. Yet to conduct this business as if it were the distribution of a simple product is wholly misleading. It is not only that the way in which education is organised can be seen to express, consciously and unconsciously, the wider organisation of a culture and a society, so that what has been thought of as simple distribution is in fact an active shaping to particular social ends. It is also that the content of education, which is subject to great historical variation, again expresses, again both consciously and unconsciously, certain basic elements in the culture, what is thought of as 'an education' being in fact a particular selection, a particular set of emphases and omissions. Further, when this selection of content is examined more closely it will be seen to be one of the decisive factors affecting its distribution: the cultural choices involved in the selection of content have an organic relation to the social choices involved in practical organisation. If we are to discuss education adequately, we must examine, in historical and analytic terms, this organic relation, for to be conscious of a choice made is to be conscious of further and alternative choices available, and at a time when changes under a multitude of pressures, will in any case occur, this degree of consciousness is vital.

Because education expresses the deep culture and political purpose of a society, choices about the service have both reflected and helped to reproduce the dominant beliefs and expectations of the society in a particular historical context: 'Education often acts as a kind of metaphor of national destinies. It seems to be a particularly appropriate vehicle for talking about the future of society in general' (CCCS 1978). The structuring of education embodies a vision of what, at a particular moment in its history, a society wishes to become over time.

Reviewing the post-war period it is possible to discern four conceptions of learning, each with its own particular emphases and choices.

Learning as child-centred development

During the 1960s, it became fashionable to talk of child-centred education, which made the development of each pupil the focus of the learning process and the centre of public policy in education. A child-centred education seeks to develop the personal qualities and capacities of each individual. To educate, according to this perspective, is to bring out, to unfold, to develop. There is a distinctive teleology underlying such a conception of education. Individuals grow and develop in a way which unfolds their inner potential. The task of education is to foster that potential so as to realize the powers and capacities of each individual. The learning process, by encouraging the individuality of each young person, is designed to facilitate independence in thought and action. The keyword in child-centred education is 'progress': learning is evaluated according to the amount of potential achieved.

Educators committed to these purposes usually stress the process of learning. Learning, it is argued, is secured more effectively through experience rather than by didactic presentation of bodies of knowledge. Active participation by students in their own learning does more to awaken the imagination. Knowledge is rooted more firmly in self-discovery than in the passive reception of formal teaching. Students are encouraged to negotiate their learning needs at each stage drawing upon teachers as resources for learning rather than as omnipotent sources of knowledge.

The idea of a child-centred education, serving the individual needs of each child, came to influence government policy-making on the aims and purposes of schooling. The 1943 White Paper proposed that 'the keynote of the new system will be that the child is the centre of education' while the Green Paper in 1977, *Education in Schools*, which summarized the 'great debate' on education, began its objectives for schools in a familiar way: 'to help children develop lively, enquiring minds, giving them the ability to question and to argue rationally, and to apply themselves to tasks'. (DES 1977:6). The paradigm statement of child-centred education, however, was made by the Plowden Committee on Primary Schools:

> A school is not merely a teaching shop . . . It is a community in which children learn to live first and foremost as children and not as future adults . . . The school sets out deliberately to devise the right environment for children, to allow them to be themselves and to develop in the way and at the pace appropriate to them. It tries to equalise opportunities and to compensate for handicaps. It lays special stress on individual discovery, on first hand experience and on opportunities for creative work. It insists that knowledge does not fall into separate compartments and that work and play are not opposite but complementary. A child brought up on such an atmosphere at all stages of his education has some hope of becoming a balanced and mature adult and of being able to live in, to contribute to, and to look critically at the society of which he forms a part. Not all primary schools correspond to this picture but it does represent a general and quickening trend.
>
> (DES 1967)

Creative self-expression fostered by the 'informal' methods of the Plowden primary school would not neglect the traditional virtues of the old elementary school – 'neatness, accuracy, care and perseverance, and the sheer knowledge which is an essential of being educated' – but rather, provide a 'much firmer foundation for their development'.

Learning as vocational preparation

By the early 1970s, accelerating unemployment led many employers to criticize what young people were learning at school. Many industrialists argued that schools were too self-absorbed and that they concentrated on the social development of young people at the expense of preparing them for their economic roles in industry and commerce. The challenges coincided with internal analyses by officials and HMI at the Department. Their internal memorandum, known as the Yellow Book (DES 1976), argued that the weakness of secondary education was that it under-prepared young people for employment: 'The time may now be ripe for change as the national mood and government policies have changed in the face of hard and irreducible facts'.

The call for a fundamental redirection of education required more political clout. This came from the Prime Minister. Callaghan's Ruskin speech launched a national debate which was summarized in a 1977 Green Paper that expressed concern about the limited relevance of the education service to the needs of industry and commerce:

> It was said that the school system is geared to promote the importance of academic learning and careers with the result that pupils, especially the more able, are prejudiced against work in productive industry and trade; that teachers lack experience, knowledge and understanding of trade and industry; that curricula are not related to the realities of most pupils' work after leaving school; and that pupils leave school with little or no understanding of the workings, or importance of the wealth-producing sector of our economy.
>
> (DES 1977:34)

The strategy of the Department of Education and Science to introduce a 'certificate of pre-vocational education' or the Manpower Services Commission in introducing YOP and YTS and then the Technical and Vocational Educational Initiative, all illuminated the intention of recent governments to introduce vocational relevance into the curriculum for 14- to 19-year-olds. This message was reinforced in *Better Schools*:

> It is vital that schools should always remember that preparation for working life is one of their principal functions. The economic stresses of our time and the pressures of international competition make it more necessary than ever before that Britain's work force should possess the skills and attitudes and display the understanding, the enterprise and adaptability that the pervasive impact of technological advance will increasingly demand . . . The Government believes that the linking of education and training, whatever form it takes, should have the preparation for employment as one of its principal functions.
>
> (DES 1985b:15–16)

The Department has repeatedly emphasized that control of the curriculum is central to its purpose: 'our focus must be on the strategic questions of the content, shape and purpose of the education system and absolutely central to that is the curriculum'. Attention focused on the 16 to 19 sector, largely because of its strategic location between secondary schooling and the world of work (or the prospect of unemployment). Being less hedged around by statutory constraints, it was also more amenable to policy planning and change. The point was underlined by a senior official:

> the 16 to 19 area is one of the key means of changing the educational system and of achieving the relevance we desire because it sits at the watershed between school and work. If we can do things with the new 17+ examination, that will give us an important lever to vocationalize or to revocationalize the last years of public schooling. That will be a very important, and significant, step indeed.

Learning as socialization

No one is an island. However much education attends to the particular needs of each individual part of the learning process, the leading out, it will focus upon learning to relate to, and to live with, others. In shaping the agency of the unfolding self, education necessarily shapes social relations: we develop ourselves in and through our relations with others. Education influences not sociability as such, but the scope of mutuality of persons in relation.

Education, therefore, cannot escape being a social and moral enterprise, encouraging ideas about the good of others as well as the importance of personal development. Education carries the function of initiating young people into the moral categories and social qualities expected by society, because educational institutions typically embody a vision of the good society as well as of the character and conduct expected of responsible members of such a society.

This suggests that an essential aspect of the education function lies in imparting to young people the values and virtues, understandings and rules, which it is believed they should possess. Learning, from this perspective, is as much a process of shaping and guiding as it is of internal unfolding. For Peters (1966), being educated always involves being initiated into a value-laden discourse regarding what is worthwhile; just as, for MacIntyre (1981), the good life necessarily involves not the self-centred individualism of modernity, but the process of possessing and exercising – through education – 'the virtues' of truth, justice and courage. Such virtues, MacIntyre argues, are deeply rooted in the traditions and practices of society, but stand independently of each individual. To educate is to acquire as well as to foster.

Education, therefore, typically has the function of re-presenting the values, knowledge and culture of a society to each new generation. This view of education, functioning to perpetuate the significant culture of a society, was articulated by the Robbins Committee on Higher Education:

> a function that is more difficult to describe concisely, that is nonetheless fundamental; the transmission of a common culture and common standards of citizenship. By this we do not mean the forcing of all individuality into common mould: that would mean the negation of higher education as we conceive it. But we believe it is a proper function of higher education, as for education in schools, to provide, in partnership with the family, a background of culture and social habit upon which a healthy society depends.
>
> (Robbins 1963)

To be educated is to be introduced to the culture of a society, to learn its language, know its rules of behaviour and to acquire respect for its moral codes. There is always a socializing process embodied in education. Sometimes this can be explicit, as in the way schools can function to reproduce the 'elaborate codes' of the middle class and thereby the advantages of cultural capital (Bernstein 1975; Bourdieu 1977). Sometimes the socialization process can be more explicit. One of the most celebrated treatises on education for socialization was of course Plato's *Republic*, which sought to fit children directly into their proper places in the social and moral order: 'an account of education which remains one of the Oxford English Dictionary's paradigms for the meaning of the word' (Ryan 1974:13).

Platonic notions of education not only survive but have dominated educational policy-making in recent years. Since the 1988 Education Reform Act the Government has increasingly emphasized the socialization function of learning. The National Curriculum has prescribed a distinctive selection of knowledge from a narrow historical and class tradition, while its cultural and religious selections have been disturbingly eurocentric.

Learning as selective differentiation

The National Curriculum, with its specified levels and targets, is a highly differentiated curriculum; as such, it has generated new forms and processes of differentiation in the classroom. Differentiation, however, is nothing new. In the 1960s the comprehensive school movement developed as a reaction against the crude institutional differentiation between the often lavishly resourced grammar schools and underresourced technical and secondary modern schools. It also evolved out of a recognition that young people of different social backgrounds have a great deal to learn from one another. Under this system routes were largely predetermined at 11+. There were exceptions, but in the main it was the 11+ branching point that was decisive for class selection and, therefore, for future occupational opportunities (see Halsey *et al.* 1980).

While in some instances the 11+ branching point was perpetuated through a system of banding, streaming or setting, the ideological thrust of comprehensive reorganization was quite clear: the equalizing of opportunity through the development of a more sophisticated process of differentiation that would meet the educational needs of all students including their need to share and learn from one another. From the outset, therefore, the idea of a common curriculum was central to the comprehensive project. As early as 1961 Raymond Williams (1965:174–5) outlined what he saw as 'the minimum to aim at for every educationally normal child'. While the notion of educational 'normality' begs a number of extremely important questions, Williams did succeed in producing a framework that for its time was radical in its recognition that the educational needs of students from different social backgrounds and with different aptitudes and abilities can be met within a shared curriculum framework.

For many teachers working within comprehensive schools, the prime task throughout the 1960s and 1970s was to develop this notion of a common curriculum through the practice of mixed-ability teaching. In part, this represented a negative reaction against streaming. Recent research had shown that in junior schools where streaming was practised, the grouping of students was as likely to be based on socio-economic and cultural factors as upon any reputable measure of academic ability. It was, therefore, undoubtedly perpetuating the structural inequalities within society (see Douglas 1964; Jackson 1964). There was also a growing body of professional opinion to suggest that, even if it were possible to eradicate the hidden factors from the selection procedure, streaming by ability was undesirable since it denied students an opportunity to learn from one another's differences (see Kelly 1974, 1975, 1978; Davies 1975; Wragg 1976).

Nevertheless, it is important to emphasize that mixed-ability teaching always stood in opposition to certain dominant assumptions which continued to assert themselves through the public examination system. Thus the introduction in 1963 of the Certificate of Secondary Education (CSE) ensured that more students left school with recognized qualifications, but did so by creating a two-tier system: CSE for the less academically able and the traditional General Certificate of Education (GCE) for those who might be expected to continue their formal education. This meant that older secondary school students were, almost invariably, taught in separate groups depending on whether they were to be entered for CSE or GCE. In 1972, the raising of the school leaving age from 15 to 16 produced a category of student in the 15 to 16 age group who hitherto would have left school at 15 and was now seen as presenting particular problems in terms of motivation. Again, the favoured solution was to produce specialist courses for these students, sometimes in purpose-built classrooms and workshops within a designated area of the school. The overall effect was to institute yet another branching point – this time at 14+ – for class selection and future career routes.

The announcement, in 1984, of the General Certificate of Secondary Education (GCSE) – with its single scale of assessment and its emphasis on assessment by coursework – challenged this selective process and ensured that, for many students, their educational options remained open until 16+. GCSE was not fully operationalized until 1988, by which time a much more extensive and, some would argue, intrusive national assessment system was about to be instituted. This, as originally envisaged, was to involve the assessment of all students at the ages of 7, 11, 14 and 16 with regard to subject-specific attainment targets distributed across a ten-point scale. The potential within this system of assessment – which has never been fully implemented – for differentiating between individual students is immense.

The impact of these national assessment arrangements on classroom practice and styles of teaching has been considerable and, with the heavy emphasis on coursework as a central feature of GCSE, is particularly marked in the later years of secondary schooling. This emphasis on GCSE coursework brought with it an important distinction between 'differentiation by outcome' and 'differentiation by task'. Officially sanctioned by the Secondary Examinations Council (SEC 1985) and embedded in the GCSE *General Criteria* (DES 1985a:para.16), that distinction is now inscribed in the dominant notions of good practice: 'good practice is most likely to be advanced when all members of staff are committed to the same aims: providing a broad, balanced, relevant and differentiated curriculum, and raising the standards for each of the pupils they teach' (NCC 1989:3). Differentiation, in other words, is no longer just a matter of assessing students in terms of certain measurable outcomes, but includes a serious consideration of pedagogical

processes. It is a matter of responding, through the use of appropriate teaching methods and resources, to the educational needs of
each child.

Reviewing these mechanisms of differentiation as they have developed over the last 40 years, it is important to recognize that
they have functioned both as part of the problem to which comprehensive reorganization was an attempted solution and as a further development and elaboration of the comprehensive ideal (see
Hart 1992). There are, in other words, important continuities and
discontinuities within the history of differentiation that can only be
explained in terms of different sets of values impacting upon the
education system. The mechanisms of differentiation are neither
politically neutral nor the progressive enactment of a single, political project. They are part of a complex process of contestation that
involves both the progressive equalizing of opportunity and the
continuing reintegration of old inequalities.

Continuities of underachievement in learning

While, as we have tried to show, the redirection of education at
significant times over the post-war years has reflected different
purposes for the service, there have nevertheless been underlying
continuities in the patterns of underachievement. These patterns
need to be understood, if opportunities to progress and to realize
potential are to be enhanced for all young people, but particularly
those in contexts of disadvantage.

The cause of underachievement lies in the long cultural tradition
of educating a minority. Only a few succeed because that is what
our society has preferred. Any analysis of the dominant characteristics of the educational and political systems reveals the institution-
alizing of underachievement. Young people fail to fulfil their potential
and develop their powers because of principles and assumptions
which are constitutive of the education system. None of the 'conceptions of learning' outlined above offers a serious and coherent
challenge to the totality of these assumptions:

Assumptions about who education is for Complex cultural boundaries
surround the process of learning. Education is too often regarded as
a stage in life: to be in education is to be young, to be successful
academically, and to be located within an institution, traditionally
a school. Such boundaries express a narrow conception of who
education is for, excluding most people and limiting the possibilities
of achievement.

Assumptions about the learning process Traditional conceptions of teaching and learning – an insistence on the didactic transmission of knowledge to passive and solitary individual pupils – have almost certainly diminished rather than enhanced the motivation of most young people. They have inculcated anxiety rather than joy at the prospect of learning.

Assumptions about the curriculum These assumptions have too often involved the introduction of unnecessary barriers into the experience of education: organizing learning into bounded subjects, bifurcating knowledge between theory and practice and defining 'an education' in the former as the accumulation of abstract understanding. More recently, a curriculum has been imposed upon the majority of young people which reverses this traditional emphasis and now insists upon a narrow concept of vocational preparation for work determined instrumentally by the needs of the labour market.

Assumptions about educational institutions Not only has education been institutionalized, but schools and colleges have typically been conceived as enclosed institutions controlled by their professional communities. Parents, employers or the wider community – the sources of complementary support and motivation – have usually been held at bay. The organizing rules and structures of educational institutions have, moreover, rarely been responsive to the needs of the clients they are designed to serve.

Assumptions about the organizing principles of the system The education system has been designed primarily for the purposes of differentiation and selection. Its determining principle, therefore, is more accurately described as a system of failure rather than a system of enabling, recording and celebrating achievement. Education has characteristically been a race to 11 or 16 or 18, a race to ensure entry into 'types' of education; indeed, to ensure 'an education'. It has been a race because 'an education' has been a privilege from which most are still excluded. The dominant instrumental assumptions are tied to the labour market and the education system has provided mechanisms for 'cooling people out' – or down – from education, to training, to work. Society has set limits on the numbers it has been willing to educate and, while those limits may have varied in their flexibility, the principles governing their application have remained much the same throughout the post-war era. They are the principles of social selection.

Thus an education has denied, or at best ignored, what the conditions of learning require: a sense of purpose and of commitment to, and responsibility for, personal development. Instead, for many, a pervasive sense of futility has been generated. The assumptions underlying selection are deeply inscribed in the economic, social and political transformations of our time. Our argument is that the sources of underachievement lie in the structures which have eroded the conditions for motivation: people do not take learning seriously because they are not encouraged to take their lives and capacities seriously.

If underachievement is to be arrested and the educational challenge of our times fully addressed, a more secure understanding and vision of learning will need to be developed. It is to this task that we now proceed.

AN ANALYTICAL MODEL OF LEARNING

The model of learning we present in this chapter – and exemplify in the central chapters of the book – seeks to analyse learning in terms of both its intrinsic goods and the institutional and cultural influences that shape it:

- The nature of learning: agency and capacity.
- The role of institutions in structuring learning.
- The roots of learning in cultural formation.

Learning as agency and capacity

Learning is a process of discovery that generates new understanding about ourselves and the world around us. But is that an adequate account of learning? What does it mean to learn? Is the experience of learning best characterized as an event or as a process which takes place over time? Where and when does learning most effectively take place? What are the outcomes and effects of learning and what conditions best support its unfolding? These are some of the questions that we need to resolve if we are to gain an understanding of the purposes and conditions of learning that can enhance the education of young people in some of the most disadvantaged contexts in the UK.

Learning provides a sense of discovery. Something new enters our experience through learning so as to alter what we know or can do. When we learn something about the effect of soil erosion or the puncturing of the ozone layer upon the environment then our knowledge is enlarged. When we learn to ride a bicycle for the first time, or use a word processor, the skills which develop expand our capacity to engage with the world around us. When introduced to a new concept of radiation in physics or of culture in anthropology, our understanding of the world is enhanced; and if prejudiced attitudes to particular groups or cultures can be dissolved then appreciation of others is thereby enriched.

Layers of learning

Learning proceeds through different layers: of developing understanding of discrete events or pieces of knowledge to becoming aware of ourselves as persons and then, more significantly, our growing capacity to shape ourselves and, with others, the world around us.

Discovering new knowledge, concepts, skills or attitudes, however, reflects different layers of learning. A new piece of factual information may become an additional increment in my accumulating knowledge of George Eliot's novels, or a new skill enhance my proficiency in word processing, but these are specific events. We associate learning with the deeper processes of influence upon our *understanding*. Learning helps us to discover why things are as they are and how they might become. Such understanding grows from processes of reflection that reveal the connection between things which had previously been unrecognized or opaque to us. To understand why is more significant than to know what. To learn how to explain things or events is to be able to grasp the principles which underlie and make sense of their working, and thus enable us to recognize their occurrence on some future occasion even though the surface characteristics may appear to be different.

To distinguish between knowledge and understanding deepens our grasp of the layering of learning. But the puzzles which learning resolves through understanding can, of course, vary enormously in their scope and significance. Making sense of the puzzling noise in the immersion system may resolve an irritating intrusion upon the peace of the household. But understanding a little more clearly the limits and possibilities of ourselves as persons, for example, is a different order of learning. Plumbing the depths of the self and its relationship to others can alter the shape of a character and thus the reach of its unfolding over time. Learning may at times be experienced as a specific event; yet it can, by changing how we think of and know ourselves and others, alter our horizons and thus our sense of place.

Learning to understand ourselves as persons means recognizing the complex interdependence of qualities that express what is distinctive about ourselves: not just our feelings, imagination, practical/social skills and cognitive powers, but their necessary relationships. The quality of our thinking necessarily reflects our emotional maturity as well as our abstract cerebral powers (Nussbaum 1990). Acknowledging that persons are beings rather than just the mental mechanisms of Descartes's *cogito ergo sum* has important implications for an education service which is still overly preoccupied with differentiating, ranking and selecting cognitive intelligence.

The work of Gardner (1983, 1985) and earlier of Hargreaves (1984) has begun to influence new ways of thinking about the capacities of people, encouraging recognition of the multidimensional quality of human intelligence. Rather than reducing an individual's potential to a single score on an IQ test, Gardner has reinforced understanding of the complexity of ability, including linguistic, musical, and logical/mathematical capacities, as well as spatial and bodily intelligences, and the ability to arrive at an emotional and mental sense of self and other people. An education which did not address all the intelligences would be a barren experience as, historically, too much of our education has been. The comprehensiveness of such an approach would also be revealed by recognizing the role of agency in learning. The distinctiveness of the person lies in the enacting of the qualities which define the whole.

Learning leads into action and grows out of the experience which action enables: it creates the capacity for *self-creation*. Understanding only lives and has meaning through our agency in the world. For Dewey this notion of learning expresses a philosophy of being in the world: through active experience we come to understand the world and to change it.

Thus the deeper significance of learning lies, through its forming of our powers and capacities, in our unfolding agency. The purpose and outcome of active learning may be a particular 'competence' which alters our capacity to intervene in experience. But the central purpose of learning is to enable such skills to develop our distinctive agency as a human being. Learning is becoming. It is an unfolding through which we learn not only what makes us unique – what individuates us – but how we can learn to make that distinctive agency work in the world. Learning involves becoming aware of our difference but also, significantly, how to enact its distinctiveness. Learning to develop the agency of the person is inescapably a temporal process: it takes time.

We need, therefore, to recover the Aristotelian conception of what it is to develop as a person over the whole of a life: the conception of life as it can be led (see MacIntyre 1981). This conception has a number of constituent elements: first, perceiving the life as a whole and the self as developing over a lifetime; second, the idea of life as a quest to discover the identity which defines the self; third, seeing the unity of a life as consisting in the quest for value, each person seeking to reach beyond the self to create something which is valued; fourth, to perfect a life which is inescapably a struggle, an experience of failure as well as success, in the quest to realize what is excellent.

We need to recover the Athenian ideal whereby human develop-ment requires recognizing the duality of values that are central to human development: a person is also a citizen whose responsibility to contribute to the well-being of the whole is matched by the obligation to acknowledge the freedom of its members. Autonomy depends upon the quality of co-operative interdependence that values the difference of others. The personal exercise of a virtue cannot be separated from the same person's making a world which recognizes such values.

We learn, in time, to re-create the public (political) sphere which underwrites any order of values because it creates those agree-ments which enable individuals and their relationships to grow and develop. Such agreements constitute the foundations: who is to be a member and what are the defining qualities? What are to be their rights and obligations to each other? What are to be the rules for determining the distribution of status and opportunity to develop capacities? Decisions about such matters have implications for every individual, determining the bases of identity and well-being. We fail to learn at our peril that these constitutive agreements only work *for* all if they are created *by* all. Learning to make the public world is as much about learning to create the processes which sustain it as about espousing the substantive values by which it is to take shape. Questions about who is to be involved and how those involved will participate (and when) can only be resolved together.

The bases of learning

To learn, then, is to develop understanding which leads into, and grows out of, action; to discover a sense of agency that enables us, not only to define and make ourselves, but to do so by actively participating in the creation of a world in which, inescapably, we live together. But what are the bases of such learning? What are the conditions and modes that allow us to enter upon this journey

	Bases of Learning		
	Individual	*Interpersonal*	*Public*
Layers of learning			
Understanding (minds)	Practical reason: the examined life	Expectations: ourselves and others	Values: recognizing difference
Self-creation (selves)	Motivation: agency and identity	Support: encouragement	Justice: rights and responsibilities
Social creation (communities)	Mutuality: identity	*Civitas*: co-operation	Discourse: conversation

Figure 2.1   The layers and bases of learning

of learning and sustain us on our way? In order to address these questions we shall develop our analysis of learning by examining its individual, interpersonal and public dimensions: see Figure 2.1.

The examined life – a life-lived in self-awareness and awareness of others – is the key mechanism of learning to learn and thus the key to entering the deeper layers of learning about the nature of agency. Such learning develops as practical reason, which involves: deliberation upon experience to develop understanding of the situation or the other person; judgement to determine the appropriate ends and course of action (which presupposes a community based upon sensitivity and tact); and learning through action to realize the good in practice.

Reasoning and testing ideas in this way reveals the indispensable mutuality or sociability of learning. It is not just that any competence is learnt with and through others, but that the subjectivities which define what we become as persons, and therefore our agency, are social creations. For learning to develop agency presupposes conceptions of what it is to be a person and thus understandings of what the self is to become over time and in relation to others. The understandings – of our sense of place and our promise – we all acquire socially through the mutuality of learning. By defining how the self is to unfold, the process also defines the nature and the reach of the motivation to learn.

Learning depends upon motivation and the empowering of internal rewards. Learning is inescapably a conscious activity. We may believe that we have unwittingly acquired some new knowledge, but it is not understood until we have exercised reflective energy upon it and made it our own. While some understanding may come easily, learning always involves some element of struggle to make sense of something which we have been unaware of. And, in the meaning we are giving to learning – to become a person with a distinctive agency in the world – it is never accomplished without struggle.

Learning, in this view, always takes effort and time – and thus motivation. Individuals cannot learn without the motivation to do so, without the sense that it has a purpose, and thus wanting to take responsibility for achieving the ends involved in the learning process. The motivation to learn is internal to the purpose of learning, in realizing the distinctive qualities of the self as agent. The rewards of learning are intrinsic to the process of enhancing personal capacities to standards of excellence. Extrinsic rewards, of money, power, status and prestige are contingent and subordinate and largely incompatible with the goods of the unfolding self (MacIntyre 1981). This implies something very different from 'life-long education or training', defined simply as access to institutions. Rather, it suggests a belief that an individual is to develop comprehensively throughout her or his lifetime and that this development should be accorded value and supported.

The purposive nature of learning presupposes a strong sense of identity in the learner. The purposes which grow out of learning imply a sense of self and personhood and thus the confidence to engage in the struggle of learning to create the values of the unfolding life. The identity always involves some element of struggle to make sense of something of which previously we have been unaware. In the meaning we are giving to learning – to become a person with a distinctive agency in the world – is never accomplished without struggle. The identity we develop for ourselves, however, and the motivation we have to unfold it are always acquired with and through others. Limited conceptions of ourselves, and limited expectation from others, seriously limit the motivation to learn.

The conditions for the unfolding self are thus social and political depending upon interpersonal *civitas*: my space requires your recognition and your capacities demand my support (and vice versa). This emphasis recalls Aristotle's celebration of civic friendship – of sharing a life in common – as being the only possible route for creating and sustaining life in the city. Such values, arguably, are now only to be found within that literature which emphasizes an ethic of caring and responsibility in the family and community and acknowledges the dissolution of the public as a separate (male) sphere (see Gilligan 1986; Pateman 1987; Okin 1991). It is only in the context of such understanding and support that mutual identities can be formed and the distinctive qualities of each person can be nurtured and asserted with confidence. Reflective interdependence remains the condition for autonomy and mutuality in learning.

Historically conditioned prejudices about capacity, reinforced by institutionalized discrimination, set the present limits of learning. The key to the transformation of prejudice lies in what Gadamer (1975) calls 'the dialogic character of understanding': through genuine conversation the participants are led beyond their initial positions to take account of others, and move towards a richer, more comprehensive view, a 'fusion of horizons', a shared understanding of what is true or valid. Discourse can lead to the valuing of difference. From this perspective, the possibility of mutuality in support of personal development depends on generating interpretative understanding – that is, on hermeneutic skills which can create the conditions for learning in society – in relationships within the family and the community and at work. Conversation lies at the heart of learning: learners are listeners as well as speakers; partakers of a discourse that is itself an act of social creation.

A presupposition of that discourse is openness: we have to learn to be open to difference, to allow our prejudgements to be challenged; in so doing we learn how to amend our assumptions, and develop an enriched understanding of others. It is precisely in confronting other beliefs and presuppositions that we are led to see the inadequacies of our own and so transcend them. Rationality, in this perspective, is the willingness to admit the existence of better options and to be aware that one's knowledge is always open to refutation or modification from the vantage point of a different perspective. For Gadamer, the concept of *bildung* describes the process through which individuals and communities enter a more and more widely defined community: they learn through dialogue to take a wider, more differentiated view, and thus acquire sensitivity, subtlety and capacity for judgement.

Reason emerges through dialogue with others, through which we learn not necessarily 'facts' but rather a capacity for new ways of thinking, speaking, and acting. It is Habermas (1984) who articulates the conditions for such communicative rationality as being 'ideal speech contexts' in which the participants feel able to speak freely, truly and sincerely. The conditions for this depend upon the creation of a more strenuous moral order. The values of learning, as much as the values which provide the conditions for learning (according dignity and respecting capacity), are moral values that express a set of virtues required of the self but also of others in relationship with the self. The values of caring and responsibility, upon which the confidence to learn ultimately depends, derive their influence from the authority of an underlying moral and social order. The civic virtues, as MacIntyre (1981) analyses them, establish standards against which individuals can evaluate their actions (as well as their longer 'quest'). Yet particular virtues derive meaning and force from their location within an overall moral framework (what MacIntyre calls a 'tradition'): it is the standards accepted by the moral community which provide the values by which each person is enabled to develop.

A moral order is a public creation and requires to be lived and recreated by all members of the community. Each person depends upon the quality of the moral order for the quality of her or his personal development and the vitality of that order depends, in turn, upon the vitality of the public life of the community. According to the Athenian ideal, the virtuous person and the good citizen were the same because the goods which inform a life were public virtues. The point of this historical reference is not to turn the clock back, but to emphasize that a moral order has authority only in so far as it involves induction into an open order rather than socialization into a closed tradition. The development of a moral community has to be a creative and collaborative process of agreeing the values of learning which are to guide and sustain life in the community.

The institutional structuring of learning

We have tried to put forward our view of learning as a process whereby we discover ourselves as persons and thereby act to create the contexts in which we live and work. Institutions are centrally involved in this process of structuring learning. Constituted to shape human nature – its dispositions, powers and capacities – institutions leave their mark on the identity, thinking, feeling of the person. Even the body is marked: the confidence or deference of carriage and gesture has its institutional origins. Institutions frame: they shape the horizons of their members and thus their sense of place. They mediate the relationship people have to their society through social time and space. At the same time what institutions become, the values and interests they embody, are shaped by the agency and power of those that come to control them. All institutions express these processes. Schools are clearly distinctive institutions in the formation of young lives, and exercise their shaping influence with particular intensity. In seeking to understand how schools shape the purpose and conditions of learning we develop the discussion around three key dimensions of institutions:

- practices (primary activities)
- structures (organizing and managing of decision-making)
- codes (organizing assumptions).

Institutional *practices* create the rules and procedures that establish what is expected, and also the sanctions which define the boundaries to acceptable action. Institutions typically seek to internalize in their members, through routines and rituals, appropriate beliefs and behaviour: for example, the sacraments for the congregation, the rituals of election, the school assembly. The routines of institutions, as Durkheim understood, encourage members to understand their necessary cohesion, one to another, while internalizing those values and beliefs which express their 'conscience collective'. These understandings are formalized in organizational *structures* and patterns of decision-making. Underlying the institutional practices and structures are assumptions, or *codes*, that are rarely made explicit but which profoundly affect the purposes and processes of learning. These assumptions frame and shape the orientation of an institution, establishing what is known and how it is to be interpreted and valued. It is the shared background of mutual understandings that generate the rules and procedures for establishing what is to be done.

Institutional practices

Practices form the primary activities that carry and embody a school's codes and organizing principles. A practice is a complex rule-governed activity shaped by standards of excellence:

By a practice I mean any coherent and complex form of socially established cooperative human activity through which internal to that form of activity are realised in the course of trying to achieve those standards of excellence which are appropriate to and partially definitive of that form of activity, with the result that human powers to achieve excellence and human conceptions of the ends and goods involved, are systematically extended . . . To enter into a practice is to accept the authority of those standards (of excellence) and the inadequacy of my

own performance as judged by them. It is to subject my own
attitudes, choices, preferences and tastes to the standards which
currently and partially define the practice.

(MacIntyre 1981:175–7)

Human qualities (for example, truth, courage, honesty) are developed through the exercise of and participation in the virtues
that define a practice. Excellence means subordinating ourselves to
the criteria, the rules and the authority of relationships within the
practice. Practices sustain institutions through the exercise of the
virtues they require.

For Bourdieu (1990), practices, deriving from the interplay between the pressure of structures and the creative improvization of
the actors' purposes, create and are re-created by an institutional
habitus: the system of durable dispositions that shape the working
of the institution. Practices are the intersection of structure and
action, of society and individual. Practices capture the practical competence which agents often have while grounding that practice
socially.

Within schools a number of distinctive educational practices shape
the processes of teaching and learning: the practices, for example,
of curriculum design, of teaching, of assessing progress in learning,
or of grouping pupils, all involve coherent social activities shaped
by rules and expected standards of excellence. These practices can
serve to integrate the processes of learning across the school or, on
the other hand, to differentiate young people into separate compartments of learning: see Figure 2.2. This way of conceptualizing
school practices offers a framework for further analysis and discussion, provided a number of points are borne in mind: first, each
dimension represents a gradation of institutional practice, not a set
of stark alternatives; second, a school may be located at several
different points along a single dimension in different areas of its
practice; third, a school may also vary significantly across dimensions in terms of the extent of 'integration'. The central chapters of
this book apply the framework outlined in Figure 2.2 to specific
school contexts with a view to analysing the underlying codes of
innovative educational practice.

We would expect what we will come to call in the chapters to
follow, 'the learning school', to develop distinctive values and institutional practices which integrate rather than separate out the
learning experience of young people. The very social constitution
of the school will embody a comprehensiveness which celebrates
the equality of difference and avoids any form of social, cultural or

−	Integration		+
Selective	School social structure		Comprehensive
Extrinsic/Instrumental	Values		Intrinsic
Individualism	Ontology	Interdependence	
Inward	Orientation		Outward
Selective	Grouping		Mixed ability
Passive/didactic	Teaching		Active/construction
Acquisition	Methods		Enquiry
Controlled	Content		Negotiated
Routine	Tasks		Complex
Restricted	Relationships	Collaborative	
Inflexible	Organization		Participative
Monolinear	Curriculum		Multilinear
Subject	Focus		Student
Outcomes	Orientation		Process
Ethnocentric	Reference		International
Information	Aims		Understanding
Summative	Assessment		Formative
Outcome	Differentiation		Task
Examination	Methods		Coursework
Fixed	Criteria		Uncertain
Classification	Purpose		Diagnosis
Standards	Attainment		Progression
Exclusive	External relations		Partnership

Figure 2.2 Conceptualizing school institutional practices

intellectual selection. A form of education will be encouraged which values learning for its own sake and is centrally concerned with the development of the whole child; it will promote learning to develop autonomy within co-operative relationships rather than possessive individualism; and it will support learning to develop the confidence of young people to reach out beyond the local and familiar to engage with worlds unknown.

The learning, comprehensive school will encourage practices which strive – through strategies of grouping, pedagogy and curriculum design – to integrate the learning process. All children are of equal worth and deserve equal opportunities; however, children are different and their needs show considerable divergence, thus effective classroom practice starts with the needs of the individual children. The learning school will favour mixed ability rather than selective groupings, preferring strategies of differentiated learning (to be discussed in Chapter 3) to allow students at different stages to learn together but also at a pace which stretches their abilities. Approaches to teaching and learning will be developed to support active learning, rather than mere memorizing, in which students are able to negotiate choices of learning that require them to take responsibility for tasks which challenge their understanding and experience. Experiment and imagination are encouraged above mere routine learning, while a range of co-operative learning practices are supported, in pairs, group work as well as whole-class activity. The learning school avoids excessive reliance on any one particular form of learning to ensure variety as well as appropriateness of experience. Continuity and progression will be ensured for each child, supported by the highest expectations.

A multilinear curriculum, encouraging breadth and variety of learning, will focus upon the needs of the learner as well as the demands of the subject, thus providing multiple forms of learning. It will emphasize understanding above accumulation of knowledge. Guidance and counselling will provide support for the learner while profiles and records of achievement will both provide positive feedback and challenge the progress which the learner is making. Close consultations with parents is essential, based on a recognition of them as prime educators in their own right.

Institutional structures

Institutional structures are not just external to individuals, they are implicated in the motives and reasons that individuals have for what they do. To create structure is not, therefore, simply a matter of translating individual intention into practice. It is a matter, rather, of gathering a multiplicity of diverse intentions, interests and dispositions in such a way as to confer support for certain kinds of activity and to authorize particular forms of interaction. Similarly, to restructure is not simply to replace one set of practices by another, but to alter the meanings that have accrued around those practices. Structure, as Giddens (1984) suggests, is better thought of as a continuing process of 'structuration', whereby structural properties are carried in reproduced practices and serve to bind those

Dimensions	Codes 'systemness'	
Strategy	*Ad hoc* ———————	Coherence
Organization	Differentiation————	Integration
Participation	Hierarchy —————	Collegiality
Professionality	Specialization————	Public service
Orientation	Extrinsic —————	Intrinsic
Boundary	Closure —————	Permeability
Relations	Competition ————	Partnership

Figure 2.3   The organization and management of
learning contexts

practices across varying spans of time and space. Structure is what gives practice its meaning and endeavour its social cohesion.

Structures embody the shared codes and dispositions which actors constitute and reconstitute through their practices. They constrain, but they also enable by conferring support for certain kinds of activity and authorizing particular forms of interaction. In Figure 2.3 we set out a framework to help understand and analyse approaches to institutional management. The code underlying the dimensions expresses the value of 'systemness' in the management of schools. Modern systems (Giddens 1977; Archer 1979) develop a capacity to reflexively interpret their changing context so as to manage their development and sustain the coherence of their internal working in pursuit of shared purposes.

The task of management is to enable those strategic choices which clarify, reinforce and structure the defining purposes of an institution. Strategy derives from an analysis of the changing context of the institution so as to determine its 'basic long term goals and objectives . . . and the adoption of courses of action and the allocation of resources necessary for carrying out those goals' (Chandler 1962). The choices about the sense of strategic direction for a school will reflect its guiding values and purposes, together with a view of the priorities it must select in the face of constrained resources. A school which adopts strategic planning, proactively shaping its way forward, is more likely to be coherent in the way it works as an institution rather than if it tended to muddle through and only reviewed its purposes in *ad hoc* reaction to the pressure of events.

How institutions frame their work and decision-making can significantly influence the degree of coherence they can achieve. Encouraging the interdependence of roles and collegiality of decision-making can reinforce the integration of a school which an overemphasis on divided roles and hierarchy can undermine. The new management of schools also believes that strong institutions do not hide behind high boundary walls of separate and specialist knowledge but recognize the need to learn about the changing world in which they live across open and permeable boundaries. Parents, communities, and other institutions are valued as partners rather than competitors.

While one school will emphasize a pattern of differentiation – through, for example, departmental autonomy, hierarchy, professional specialization and boundary maintenance – another will strive for integrated working through, say, whole-school development planning, collegiality, boundary permeability, and public-service orientation.

Institutional codes or organizing assumptions

Underlying the institutional practices of schooling are organizing assumptions that are rarely made explicit but which profoundly affect the processes and purposes of learning. These underlying assumptions shape the orientation of an institution, establishing what is known and how what is known is to be interpreted and valued. They ensure that the power of an institution resides less in its ability to regulate and more in its capacity to generate and re-create the provinces of meaning by which its members interpret and make sense of their worlds. It is these assumptions that generate rules and procedures for establishing what is to be expected, the sanctions which define the boundaries to acceptable action.

Bernstein's (1975) thesis on educational codes provides a helpful starting point for understanding the way educational institutions in general, and schools in particular, work to structure learning. He proposed that the educational experience of young people is shaped by curricula which define what is to count as valid knowledge and by pedagogic processes that determine acceptable forms for the transmission of knowledge. Underlying and unifying the message systems of curriculum and pedagogy are principles or codes which regulate the structure of knowledge ('classification') and the processes of transmission ('framing'). Classification, referring to the extent of differentiation and insulation of curricula contents, focuses attention upon the forms of power which maintain and reproduce the boundaries between categories. Framing, on the other hand, refers to the context in which knowledge is transmitted and, by defining the principles which regulate what may be transmitted, focuses upon the underlying principles of control. The strength of classification and framing, and their relationship to each other, reveals the underlying codes of meaning and power: power and control are made substantive in the classification and framing procedures which shape educational contexts and practices.

Bernstein's typology of educational codes – 'collection' and 'integrated' – and the historic shift he discerns between these two codes can be used to illuminate the changing pedagogic practices of schools in producing different kinds of citizen. The collection code finds its purest expression in the subject bias of the National Curriculum. The purity of specialized knowledge is protected not only through the maintenance of subject boundaries but also through the ordering of pupils who, streamed and graded, must demonstrate capacity by passing through ritual examinations to attain selected membership of more advanced stages. A divided curriculum is a controlled curriculum. The integrated code, on the other hand, is characterized by an openness which blurs the boundaries between subjects, thereby shifting the emphasis from knowledge as isolated compartments to the notion of curriculum contents standing in a necessary interrelationship and requiring to be open to each other.

Whereas collection codes rest upon strength of boundary (and thus upon the controlled access to knowledge), integrated codes depend upon collectivity and consensus (and thus upon control exercised through interpersonal relationships). The opening of the boundaries of knowledge requires and stimulates the opening of organizational boundaries, as teachers and pupils are required increasingly to extend relationships across hierarchical and disciplinary divisions. Altered conceptions of knowledge and of its transmission may well bring about a disturbance in the structure and distribution of power. For example, the weaker framing of integrated codes increases the potential influence and participation of students in the learning process, but this is at the expense of student privacy, which becomes eroded as more of the students' capacities and attributes are given over to learning. Similarly, the weaker classification of integrated codes reduces the control of teachers, as didactic styles give way to co-operative styles. Integrated codes, therefore, as Bernstein suggested, may generate a trend towards a common system of transmitting and evaluating educational knowledge and will certainly presuppose a high level of ideological consensus without which shared commitment to the system is likely to founder.

Under a collection code it is only the academic élite who, socialized through successive levels of bounded knowledge, are admitted finally to the realization that knowledge itself is provisional and socially constructed. Under curricula generated by an integrated code, however, the teaching process begins with this understanding, seeking to encourage all young people to explore more openly the principles of knowledge creation. Implicit in the shift from collected to integrated code is the focus upon the student and her or his learning needs and difficulties. The notion of an integrated code is useful for our purposes in so far as it enables us to distinguish between sets of practices on the basis of their underlying principles. Activities are loaded with significance and need to be decoded if we are to make sense of them.

Cultural formation and the roots of learning

We have considered the nature of learning and the role of institutions in structuring learning. But what of the roots of learning within the cultural formation of the child? To what extent, and in what ways, does culture form and shape the outcomes and processes of learning?

Culture can be seen as an apparatus whereby the élite inevitably reproduce the conditions of their own élitism while the disadvantaged spiral into ever greater depths of deprivation. But culture cannot be explained entirely in terms of this heavily deterministic model of reproduction. It is always unpredictable in its outcomes; the principles of structuration as articulated, for example, by Giddens (1984) and implicit in Bauman's work (1973) show why this is the case. Culture is never just a given feature of the social environment in which individuals exist, but involves also, always, an element of agency that allows for the possibility of groups and individuals bucking the system: I am not just the product of my cultural origins; I am a beginning.

It is the work of Bourdieu (1990) that is most valuable in avoiding the problems of cultural determinism. His perspective is one which transcends the dichotomies of determinism and freedom, conditioning and creativity, consciousness and unconsciousness, the individual and society. The human condition, as Bourdieu sees it, is as remote from the creation of totally unpredictable novelty as it is from simple mechanical reproduction. As Bourdieu himself makes clear, it is institutions that perform the main mediating function: 'an Institution . . . is complete and fully viable only if it is durably objectified not only in things, that is in the logic, transcending individual agents, of a particular field but also in bodies, in durable dispositions' (p.58). So, while institutions reproduce conditions, cultures and values, they do so in relatively unpredictable ways; and that relative unpredictability is all in the agency.

So, while the nature of learning – as progression towards agency and the development of capacity – is always subject to institutional structuration, this process is in turn deeply shaped by, and inscribed within, the cultural formations of society. To understand learning we must grasp the cultural processes which define the notions of ability and capacity and which prescribe who should have access to particular learning opportunities. The concept of culture, however, has itself changed over time and we need to grasp something of its shifting nuances of meaning if we are to use it to inform our understanding of learning.

Culture as a whole way of life

Early post-war discussions of education and culture, particularly in the field of English studies, tended to focus on the fiercely contested notions of 'high' and 'common' culture. Support for the notion of 'high' culture rallied round T.S. Eliot's (1948) *Notes towards the Definition of Culture* with its stated thesis 'that education should help to preserve the class and to select the élite' (p.100) and was given a boost with the publication of George Steiner's (1971) *In Bluebeard's Castle: Some Notes toward the Re-definition of Culture*, which characterized contemporary life as a 'post-culture' in which the only hope for civilization lay in 'the gifted few' (p.69). It is important to remember that the post-war period in England, which is often associated with the attempt to create a new kind of egalitarianism, retained this élitist conception of culture.

This dominant understanding of culture was shaken by the work of three key figures who not only transformed their own academic fields but helped found a new one in the form of cultural studies: Richard Hoggart and his *Uses of Literacy*, E.P. Thompson with *The Making of English Working Class* and Raymond Williams with *Culture and Society 1780–1950* and *The Long Revolution* (all published between 1957 and 1963). Raymond Williams's work has perhaps had the most direct influence on the curriculum as a whole, although his early work did not begin to impact seriously on the public debate about education and culture until the second half of the 1960s. By then Williams's argument that 'a culture is not only a body of intellectual and imaginative work: it is also and essentially a whole way of life' (Williams 1958:311) was beginning to exert an influence

both within the field of English studies and within the broader and
burgeoning study of education. Furthermore, his insistence that
'working class culture' is 'a very remarkable creative acheivement'
with its own 'manners, habits of thought, and intentions' (p.313)
had a profound effect on a new generation of teachers deeply committed to the ideals of comprehensive schooling. For that generation of teachers the idea that culture is always something that is
being lived – and, therefore, 'always in part unknown, in part un-
realised' (p.320) – was taken as an invitation to rethink many of the
pedagogical and curriculum assumptions underlying the education
system.

Culture as contestation

Such a stance could, and in certain quarters did, lead to the senti-
mentalizing of working-class culture. Williams's own trail, however, led in a very different direction. Throughout the 1970s he
became increasingly concerned with the relation between culture
and historical change and with the role of the 'dominant culture'
within the change process (see Williams 1977, 1980). He analysed
the workings of the dominant culture in terms of 'the way in which
from a whole possible area of past and present, certain meanings
and practices are chosen for emphasis, certain other meanings and
practices are neglected and excluded'. The dominant culture is 'built
into our living' as a set of presuppositions that present themselves
to us as a seemingly uncomplicated 'selective tradition' (1980:39).
Withstanding that tradition and thereby resisting the dominant
culture means continually thinking against the grain.

   The idea of culture as contestation is the main legacy left by the
long and still unresolved wrangle over the definition of culture as
either 'high' or 'common', and continues to inform the more recent
post-modernist debate on cultural change (see Rutherford 1990).
That debate is constructed around issues of power and pluralism:
dominance not as a single, centrifugal force, but as a confusing push
and pull of ideological pressures operating on the individual within
an increasingly fragmented cultural space. It is a debate in which
traditional notions of social class have lost out to questions of identity and difference, and where those questions are increasingly posed
in terms of gender and ethnicity (see, for example, Hall 1990 and
Giddens 1991, 1992). Culture, from this perspective, is constantly
forming and reforming around the interests of the identities that
comprise and are comprised by it.

Culture as symbolic classification

We see culture as a complex process of symbolic classification, which invariably operates tacitly and whose effect, therefore, is never fully apparent. We take from the post-modernist debate an understanding of the shifting, indeterminate relation between identity and culture: identity does not come ready-made as part of a defined cultural heritage; rather, it is the arduous outcome of a process that involves constant positioning and repositioning. Increasingly, identity is a 'project' that is conducted, not within or between clearly delineated cultural boundaries, but within a cultural 'space' that is already ideologically overcrowded and where everyone is on the move (see Bauman 1992). Learning is not something that happens once an identity has been formed: it is central to the process of cultural formation.

That process operates at a number of levels. At one level it serves to distinguish the *moral order*: the identity of self and others; the distinction between private and public; the line between sacred and profane. At another level it marks the boundaries of the *social order*: differentiating 'us' from 'them'; inner from outer; inclusion and exclusion. At a third level it constitutes the values underlying the *political order*: the relations of power; of super- and subordination; of state and nation; of membership of the polity. It is in the complex workings of this process of cultural formation that difference is at once assimilated into the deep structures of classification; structures which, by their own dialectic, must in turn accommodate themselves to the emergence of diverse cultural identities.

Such a perspective has led some writers to proclaim a new 'politics of identity', which Shotter (1993) has suggested must be a politics of both 'identity and belonging': a politics of difference *and* of community (see also Phillips 1991, 1993). We would see our work as contributing to such a politics, but in a quite specific way: through the development of a theory of learning that is grounded in the organizational and managerial realities of school life and in the social and cultural complexities of becoming a learner. We are interested, ultimately, in how schools manage in contexts of disadvantage and what messages may be taken from these schools for more general application to other contexts and sites.

In the following two chapters we set about the task of applying some of the theoretical insights developed in this chapter to the work of particular schools located in contexts of disadvantage. The focus of the two chapters differs: Chapter 3 is primarily concerned with pedagogical, curriculum and assessment issues; Chapter 4 with the social and institutional conditions of schooling. Both chapters, however, are centrally concerned with learning. Our argument is that the organizing principles of the effective school are, first and foremost, principles for complex, purposeful learning; principles, that is, that can challenge the underlying assumptions and practices of the institution and thereby call the institutional structures to account.

THREE

The learning school I

In the previous chapter we conceptualized learning in terms of the processes and conditions which enable individuals to develop their agency and realize their capacities. The deeper layers of learning begin to unfold when we begin to learn about the creation of the self as being necessarily connected to the creation of a world not yet finished. The conditions that sustain this layered progression – what we call the bases of learning – are at once individual, interpersonal and public. Individual motivation, for example, relies at the interpersonal level on supportive encouragement, and both in turn presuppose a public domain in which rights and responsibilities are upheld through open debate. Both the processes and conditions of learning tend, in other words, towards the realization of a civic society in which the individuation of the self is an inescapably social and indeed public affair. Such a society we would define as a learning society. Our aim in this and the following chapter is to articulate the codes, practices and institutional structures of schools which express these values of active learning so that they become 'learning schools'.

In this chapter we explore the practices of learning – through pedagogy, curriculum and assessment – that support the unfolding agency of young people. Underlying these practices, we have argued, are certain codes – or sets of tacit assumptions – that profoundly influence the experience of learning. Practices will develop very different meanings and embody different experiences according to the values and beliefs that inform them. Ostensibly different practices, however, may be united by the same driving values and purposes. A particularly important distinction for us in the coding of practices is the extent to which practices differentiate or integrate young people in their personal development in relation to each other as well as to traditions in the community. The learning school will strive to recognize differences and to dissolve boundaries between them.

The schools we have studied have sought to alter their purposes and forms of learning, acknowledging that the key to motivating young people to become active learners with a sense of purpose within and beyond the school grows out of recognizing, valuing and accommodating the complex and different identities they have as persons. We explore the shifting purposes of the learning school at a number of levels:

- value-driven learning
- integrative practice:
  pedagogy: an emphasis on active learning
  curriculum: towards a student-centred curriculum
  assessment: formative and positive assessment
- codes of cognitive differentiation.

Value-driven learning

The learning school is driven by values. Values are carefully chosen in the learning school to celebrate a distinctive vision about the reservoirs of capacity in individuals: the purpose of education being to create active rather than passive learners, empowered with the skills to make responsible choices about the direction of their own lives as well as to co-operate with others to improve the quality of life for all in the community. The learning school values:

The identity and dignity of each   'First and foremost among these fundamental values – the non-negotiables if you like – are the equal valuing of people and the importance of developing all aspects of a person'. Education helps young people to form positive attitudes to themselves as well as others and thus to dissolve prejudice. Young people are encouraged in the learning school to value difference and diversity within and between communities. All need to develop understanding, respect and tolerance for other cultures and religions, recognizing that all contribute to the quality of life in the community. As one headteacher said:

> We believe in welcoming students from all backgrounds. We are very multicultural and we actually considered changing the name of the school to 'The International School' because we have got so many countries represented. Our language survey

showed that 34 languages other than English were spoken. We promote bilingualism and multilingualism in our school. It's seen very much as a high skill and a very worthwhile skill. This international flavour to our school comes through, both in the curriculum and in the way people are welcomed into the school: this is very important to us.

Learning can help pupils to make sense of cultural values and the way in which they are expressed in our society.

Individual capacity and achievement 'We believe that no limit should be assumed to the individual's capacity for achievement. This must be the basis of expectations of all children and young people from all backgrounds'. Believing in the considerable capacities of young people and their potential across all the areas of experience is a precondition for learning and achievement: 'Because the kids come from a deprived area, from an area of high unemployment or from an area where there is high crime and poor housing stock, it does not mean to say that they have got to come into an institution like this and put up with a second-rate version of themselves'. One head remarked on the wide-ranging talents of young people and that an education should enable them to develop the variety of these capacities: aesthetic and creative, ethical and spiritual, social and sporting as well as academic. Wealth of capacity leads to richly endowed young people. The learning school recognizes and reinforces the multidimensional quality of human capacities:

- aesthetic and creative: capacity for being creative and appreciating the creation of others
- linguistic and literary: capacity to make meaning through talking and writing
- mathematical: logical capacities to identify, classify and measure numerical patterns
- scientific: capacity to analyse ourselves, material forces and the living environment
- moral: capacity for judging the right, the fair and just, for awareness of and living with others
- spiritual: capacity for awe, wonder, and the significance of life
- physical: capacity to create a healthy life
- human and social: capacities to understand and create relationships with others.

Recognizing capacity allows achievement to be recognized and celebrated and thus confidence to grow.

Assertiveness and self-confidence   Self-dignity and confidence are not only important educational values in their own right but also an essential basis for personal development and progress in learning. To learn is to reach out, to examine something beyond the self and to encounter a different environment and the strangers within it. One head stressed the significant value of

> developing a self-confident person, who is able to commun-
> icate with others both known and strangers in different envir-
> onments. And I include in this, going out into the world, mixing
> with others, and being able to project and stand up for them-
> selves: to be confident and therefore go on to achieve whatever
> they wish to do.

This value of self-confidence is especially important for groups which have, traditionally, been disadvantaged by education. Girls, for example, need to become more assertive if they are to fulfil their learning capacities both within and beyond school:

> We want girls to be proud of being female and be aware that
> they can enter any profession they wish and that they can play
> a major role both in school and in the world outside. This
> school wishes to ensure that girls will leave equipped with the
> skills to speak up for themselves, to be assertive and to ques-
> tion . . . You have this history of girls being passive and being
> seen as well behaved and 'very good students' because they
> sit in a corner and read and copy out. But when they are
> actually tested on paper they can do poorly. I think passivity is
> a great danger. Girls, unfortunately, have a history of being
> told to shut up while the male speaks, whatever culture they
> come from. We have got to build up the self-esteem and self-
> confidence of girls.

Confidence in language is a key educational value. Many schools are promoting bilingualism as an intrinsic value but also as an essen-tial support to progress for the black and ethnic minorities:

> It is important to promote and welcome bilingualism because
> it is a vital skill and also because it is an asset that improves the
> self-confidence of the bilingual speaker. That confidence then
> permeates that person's experience around other areas of the
> curriculum. Research has shown that if a person can actually
> think through concepts in their own language then they will
> make the steps and acquire those concepts. So it is important

to be in an environment that encourages you and makes you feel comfortable to think and speak in your own language.

Empowerment for autonomy and responsibility   Empowerment enables children to become independent learners: to manage what they are doing, make decisions about the best way of doing it and have access to resources. To achieve this students need to become knowledgeable, skilled and critically aware: 'we believe that schools should help students to achieve the maximum control over their lives'; 'an education should develop the potential young people have to think and act for themselves':

> I think education is about equipping students to be able to exercise as much control over their lives in the future in both the public and private capacity. And this means giving them skills and knowledge and experience . . . I guess exams to some extent are part of this but I think it's also about giving self-confidence and self-esteem and about trying to encourage them to become caring and responsible individuals with a critical awareness of the world about them.

Language is seen by many as the means through which young people can be empowered by the learning process. Language means literacy. But literacy is far more than a basic skill: it enables young people to create meaning. Literacy as control of meaning empowers the student as a writer, a reader and a person. By enabling communication it creates the fundamental tool of awareness and provides the capacity for choice and the shaping of a life:

> One of the things they need is effective literacy, and they also need to know how to find information and know-how to challenge that information, not just to take everything as read, believing that it's true just because 'I saw it on the telly, or I read about it'. They need to learn to question and challenge their history in particular: they have to learn to ask whose history, what history, whose benefit is it to write this down? What's missing and what's not there? All those questions apply to adult life.

Developing such competencies enables young people to acquire an increasing sense of self-reliance, integrity and flexibility to face changing circumstances.

Taking responsibility for others and the wider community   The learning school wishes to encourage an outward-looking education: 'schools

and colleges should help young people to form constructive and co-
operative attitudes to each other, to their work and to the community so that they can play an active and responsible role as citizens
in society'. Can opportunities be made available for students to
assist in supporting the learning of others, perhaps adults as well as
younger pupils? Can students take responsibility for the quality of
appearance of their own school?

By taking responsibility for others and the wider community young
people learn to acknowledge their interdependence as a potential
source of wealth which is generated through co-operative action.
To this end young people need to be encouraged to participate
within the school and the community. They are empowered to
make decisions and this requires learning to accept responsibility
for them. The learning school helps young people to learn how to
take decisions because the learning processes which are involved in
that are paramount for a successful life. Encouraging ownership in
decision-making is important as a vital process of learning about
developing autonomy and responsibility:

> We need to understand what making a decision is: we make a
> decision about crossing the road, what we eat, the bases of life.
> Yet from very early on many decisions are made for us. We
> have to help young people to learn how to take decisions, to
> learn about taking responsibility. We have to support people
> through making the wrong decisions; it is only in that way that
> they can learn. Without the advantage of support and practice
> they will continue to fail. But in managing a coffee bar or a
> play scheme, or in planning a school trip, young people can
> learn to take decisions, handle responsibility, and if they are
> successful at this level they can proceed with more confidence
> to take more serious decisions. Our role is to support people in
> this process of understanding the complexities of decision-
> making. If we have the community owning what is in the
> community, our problems of theft and vandalism, disregard
> etc. will diminish because people will think that what is in the
> community – shops etc. – are theirs: they will have respons-
> ibility for it, they will have responsibility to encourage other
> people to respect it, other people, and property.

Public education to empower the local community is important
because it is only the experience of making decisions that generates
real understanding of how institutions and government work, as
well as responsibility in relation to them. Community education,

therefore, seeks to develop the powers and capacities of individuals and groups to enable them to participate together as citizens to develop understanding of their mutual needs and to take responsibility for the development of the community as an accountable democracy. A learning public will enable an educated democracy.

Integrative practice

The learning school is characterized by pedagogical, curriculum and assessment practices which express the values we have outlined above. These practices strive to integrate the learning process through: *active learning* strategies whereby students are able to negotiate choices of learning that require them to take responsibility for tasks that are intrinsically challenging and enjoyable; a *student-centred curriculum* that respects individual differences while building on the strengths of the local community; and a system of *positive assessment* that provides individual feedback within a context of care and support.

Active learning

If learning is to be effective it should motivate young people by engaging their interests and by relating to their experience. The process of teaching, moreover, should seek to involve students in, and negotiate with them, a process of active and collaborative learning: 'We must shift from a teaching approach to a learning approach'. The practices emphasize:

Student-centred learning Education should begin from the needs and strengths of the individual and not merely the benchmarks of preconceived standards: 'Learning should be appropriate to the needs of individual pupils and provide a challenge to each one'. Engaged, purposeful learning requires of the teacher a willingness to listen to students so as to find the best ways of motivating them.

> I strongly believe in the importance of involving the child in its own learning. Learning is a vulnerable and difficult experience: the child may find it difficult to know what question to ask so that their difficulty can be sorted out. We need to listen closely to children and that would tell us quite a lot. We need to take time and involve them, to share the ownership of learning. It does not help when 'the problem' of learning is ours and we

tell children the answers. It is only when the child owns the problem of learning, recognizes that learning is important to them, that they will then be really motivated to 'want to write' or 'to read'.

A recent study of 'reluctant learners' in one LEA suggested that they wanted more involvement, ownership and consultation: 'they wanted to be listened to'. An engaged student is more likely to understand and to become motivated. The quality of learning in the classroom depends upon the capacity of teachers to listen. From the quality of their openness and trust, self-confidence and motivation can develop:

> I want to get back to that question you asked before about what you can do about young people who feel really bad about themselves. I've got a lovely example – a young lad who's in our first year. He and I didn't see eye to eye for quite a while and I was responding to him in a way that I knew I ought not to be. He was antagonizing me and I was antagonizing him. I was teaching with a colleague at the time and she said, 'He's difficult, that Martin: I have to really bite my tongue sometimes.' I'd seen her with him and she did bite her tongue and she was good with Martin and it forced me to try again. Gradually there were things Martin began to tell me – after a great deal of discussion. Martin hadn't felt safe talking about those things with me and that was why I was not getting very far. But gradually the relationship got better, even if it was just a matter of my saying, 'I hear what you're saying, Martin, but where do we go from here?' Anyway, next week is half term and on Thursday night we've got a PTA [Parents and Teachers Association] jumble sale and Martin is coming to help. Martin feels good about that. He came up to me the other day and said, 'Have you done that letter for me yet, sir, to my parents to say that I'm needed on the jumble sale?' That is how bridges are built, I think. I hope. I think what Martin needs are a lot more experiences like this with lots and lots of people to make him feel good about himself. But it has started.

The important point here is that through listening, the teacher began to take what the student said seriously and, in so doing, took the student seriously. It took time, but out of the trust created emerged a regenerated and motivated student.

Participation and dialogue   As well as acknowledging both the status of the student and the motivation derived from owning the learning process, many teachers see the need to gain the student's agreement regarding what is an appropriate task for that student at that particular stage in their development: 'Successful learning experiences will stem from negotiating the learning task'. A key question for many teachers, therefore, in reflecting upon their own practice is: how far are pupils involved in the design of the learning process? Involving students through dialogue is not seen as a peripheral activity – something to be fitted in before or after the lesson – but is integral to the learning process, so that teachers in planning their lessons are thinking about how to maximize the opportunities for talking with individual students and groups of students about their progress. The involved student is likely to become a motivated and purposeful student. The learning school seeks to dissolve the boundary between teacher and student and thereby achieve a fully rounded relationship based on mutual respect and a common concern with development through learning: 'If the nature of the relationship between the teacher and the pupil is right, everything else fits into place.'

Active learning   There is a strong belief amongst teachers in disadvantaged schools that if the learning process is to be interesting and exciting, it needs to become a more active experience than was the case traditionally in most schools. The pattern, familiar to generations, of pupils sitting passively at their desk listening to a teacher and copying from the blackboard, is believed to stifle rather than encourage learning progress. To involve the pupil actively is to engage their interest, to sustain their motivation to succeed in their several courses: 'We believe in an exciting education; we want learning to be an interesting experience. We do not want to promote passivity with the teacher being the didactic giver of knowledge. We want the children to be active and encouraged to take responsibility for their own learning.'

Active learning has a number of defining characteristics: student participation, teacher negotiation, students working at their own level but on learning tasks with clear objectives for achieving progress in learning. The active learning approach is being developed in many areas of the curriculum:

- Problem-solving: 'How frequently do pupils have an opportunity to apply knowledge and understanding previously gained to the solution of appropriate problems? To what extent does such problem solving involve practical activity?'
- The performance arts: it is recognized that the performance arts can

be very important in developing the self-image and confidence of young people. In one school 11-year-olds plan a drama project to perform for a local authority, or a community centre, or in the playground. They have to negotiate with adults what is to be performed and how it is to be staged. This practical and creative approach to learning motivates the pupils and develops a wider range of skills. For a module in the performance arts, students undertake a number of activities in the arts which they develop and shape themselves using the teachers as expert resources: 'The children are given a starting point. They then develop it themselves, take it where they want to go. They use new resources, they video the performance, they watch it critically, evaluate it and try to improve it. That has been a really exciting course'.

- Independent investigation: 'The new courses encourage an active learning and a student-negotiated philosophy. There is room for the individual student to research a particular interest. We do a lot of researching, going out and meeting the public as well as inviting people into the school'. 'How frequently are pupils required to seek out information themselves by using a library or some other sort of resource bank? What steps are taken to ensure that pupils acquire appropriate techniques for such data searching? How much exploration and experimentation do pupils undertake as part of their curricular experience?'

Understanding the wider purpose and usefulness of learning 'Learning must be of significance for the pupils' future life, but should also be interesting and motivating to the particular pupil at every stage of development'. Learning can be given meaning and purpose by serving the needs of others and taking responsibility for others.

One adviser was particularly adept at considering the purposive applications of learning beyond the school in the community: 'For example, one exercise to learn about electrical circuitry asked pupils to design and test a mechanism, suitable for use in an old person's flat, that would provide warning to the warden without the old person having to activate anything'. Why is this purposive application important, it was asked?

Because it gives meaning to education; it is not doing things to please teachers; it illustrates that learning is about something useful. It shows an application of learning to help someone lead a better life. Right across the curriculum teachers should seek to relate what is happening in schools to what use can be made of it in the community. I'm not sure that it can be done all the time, but it can be achieved much more often. We must make learning more purposeful; get pupils to see learning as of some use to them and their communities. I can understand many pupils being bored with school: what use is there in it. Yet knowledge does have to be acquired: you can only apply knowledge if you have some.

Community projects are a further example of the way in which the motivation to learn may be inspired by the purpose of public service. Community Enterprise encourages young people to take control of their learning and involves them in setting up projects which will be of benefit to the community. They set themselves up as a group, identify a need and organize how they will work. 'Ice-line has been set up by students with the aid of Help the Aged. It is a project to help old people during the winter months. The students provide a telephone service; they provide an information post to put people in contact with various agencies; they provide facilities such as blankets and advice on ways to conserve heat'. Community Service illustrates how children can work with old people and the handicapped in the community as well as working in industry. 'It is the need to involve the children in the wider community: to develop pride in it; become part of it; develop a contribution to make to it'.

Collaborative learning   If students are to achieve the educational values of respecting and understanding other persons and cultures then the very process of learning needs to encourage collaborative as well as individual activity. Pupils need to be given responsibility to develop projects together, to decide the ends and plan the means. An adviser we spoke to has begun to emphasize the importance of co-operation in learning:

> There is often not enough group work in the classroom. Although children may be sitting round a table, when you look at what they are doing they are working through individualized learning schemes. So I've been encouraging and suggesting genuine group activity, starting with paired activities because particularly young children find it very hard to co-operate. They need to start with paired work and build up to undertaking group work. The importance for learning is that children feel positive about themselves and others and begin to develop confidence in a group setting. If children have a good self-image their academic work will begin to improve because making progress in learning and taking it seriously

requires confidence that it is worthwhile, has point, that effort will lead to achievement.

Students need to develop the understanding that progress in learning should be a shared activity; that we require others to contribute to our discoveries and to support our own development: learning is most fulfilling as a collaborative rather than a solitary enterprise; co-operation is more fruitful than competition. Your ideas and knowledge become the spark to my discovery: your progress is necessary to mine. The aim is to develop a style of learning that motivates and challenges students, but not by playing them off one against the other. Implicit in that aim is a rejection of the idea that learning is some kind of competitive free-for-all where the success of the few requires the failure of the many. Students are not competing against one another, nor against an abstract set of criteria. There do not have to be losers.

The public service projects we referred to above were successful not only in serving the community but also in helping young people to develop skills in working together as a team: 'They learn to develop self-awareness but also group awareness: how to identify strengths and weaknesses within the group, to agree responsibilities, to communicate and negotiate, and to resolve conflict.'

Learning as challenge   For learning to be enjoyable it must challenge and engage the student. It must involve pace, complexity and variety, but at a level that is appropriate and relevant to the student. 'We have been turning kids off science quite successfully at various levels, and this reflects the way that science has been taught. If science is made more interesting (why shouldn't it be fun?) and relevant then learning will be stimulated and supported.' Education can be an enjoyable and worthwhile experience in its own right: 'the acid test of a good curriculum is whether it is exciting as well as demanding serious hard work'. The teaching methods that are used should reflect this concern with learning as an experience that is at once enjoyable and challenging: 'Too many schools are still boring, dull environments with the teachers providing information and notes being made. Schools must develop more exciting, stimulating varied learning experiences. There may be a place for information-giving but there must be a much greater variety of approaches.' Young people need to be introduced to a variety of teaching approaches if they are to make of their own learning something that is intellectually challenging and enjoyable: 'Schools should arrange for their pupils to have opportunities to learn in a variety of models. Individual pupils may vary in their response to teaching methods, and wherever possible should be given some choice about how they learn. Traditional didactic techniques certainly have their place, but should not be the general rule'.

A student-centred curriculum

Careful organization and planning of the learning experience – both the timetabled as well as the 'hidden' curriculum – are regarded as vital to providing opportunities to all young people to develop their capacities and expand their powers of autonomy and citizenship. A student-centred curriculum is:

A relevant curriculum Learning should connect with the experience of the pupils and be perceived as relevant to their learning and development. Young people are more likely to make sense of the learning when they can make sense of the content and process of learning and when they can relate it to life within the community: 'Children and young people must perceive that the curriculum offers what they need; that it relates as much as possible to the world in which they live'; 'We must look at what is going on in the community, in children's lives and make the curriculum relevant to their lives.'

The learning school seeks to break down the boundary between the institution and the community. The task is: 'How can you relate the curriculum – the experience of children in school, what goes on inside school – to what goes on outside. [The purpose is] to enable what goes on outside to impact on the curriculum in a real sense; [to bring] . . . people in to really begin to address issues which affect the school.' An adviser argued strongly that education should help to develop all young people as citizens so that they can play a full role in a democratic society:

> In the past, science courses have been aimed at those who would eventually be the 1 per cent and get a science degree. Now we aim at 100 per cent who will eventually be citizens in an increasingly scientific and technological world that they have to make . . . They need to understand the arguments about the greenhouse effect . . . they need to be scientifically aware because how can they take part in a democratic society if they do not understand what the arguments are?

Learning is recognized as occurring in the community as well as within the school: 'Use the curriculum to develop understanding of

the community. Spend time in the community centres, perhaps a
Hindu Temple, an old persons home, or a special needs school to
develop a wider understanding of the whole community.' One school
is committed to the idea that the quality of learning and of life
in the community must be perceived by the school as mutually
enriching. By enriching the curriculum through environmental
studies and performance arts it is building new confidence, skills,
social abilities and creative imagination. It is mistaken to see the
'academic' and the 'community' as separate: 'they feed into each
other'. The environmental work of the students is providing the
motivation for formal learning; it is also practically protecting the
local environment and, in so doing, showing the students the possibility of reclaiming and transforming the environment. This 'is very
important for human survival'.

A comprehensive curriculum   Developing all the powers and capacities of the individual for the responsibilities of citizenship requires a
comprehensive curriculum of social, cultural, practical and political
education as well as cognitive development. The learning school
seeks to break down the barriers between subjects in the learning process: 'We are not just concentrating on the cognitive aspects
of personal development here, although traditionally that is what
schools are about. We are looking at the development of the whole
child. I actually believe that is very, very important'. Students introduced to a broad curriculum which encourages all the aspects of
learning – knowledge, concepts, skills and attitudes – are more
likely to acquire the diversity of skills necessary to develop autonomy as well as to enjoy a more interesting learning experience.
Teachers and advisers seek to develop broad and balanced opportunities for students to enrich their experience through social, environmental and outdoor education which uses the community and
supports learning about it.

An integrated and coherent curriculum   The learning experience should
not be experienced as fragmentary. Rather, one aspect of the curriculum should always be perceived as related to and illuminating
others. Separate courses and the curriculum as a whole should be
characterized by coherence: 'Pupils should be able to see the aims
of the curriculum and the priorities of the school and the LEA
within their learning programmes'. What matters is not coherence
in the abstract, but coherence in the experience of the student: the
extent to which the curriculum adds up and makes sense to the
student in terms of her or his own aspirations and conditions.

A comprehensive curriculum becomes unified by the integrating themes of citizenship: gender and race, multiculturalism, work and power in society, and so on. Water, for example, involves a number of subject areas such as geography, science, history, English and social studies. 'There are a number of connecting issues surrounding water: who owns it? How is it distributed? How do you get access to it? How do you make sure it is clean? What happens to communities if they haven't got access to clean water?' This form of teaching helps to develop in students a much greater awareness of issues to do with economics, power, social structure and gender (for example, who fetches the water). They are local issues as well as world issues at the present time. Such teaching is part of the process of helping to empower young people, 'by which I mean helping children and other people to take control over their own lives'. The prime task is to help young people to unify their lives, not to engender or compound a sense of fragmentation.

Cross-curricular working is believed to be vitally important. 'We need to get teachers talking to each other, producing units of work together and looking at how they can teach it. This collaborative process has begun to take place. Schools need to examine the constraints upon integrated working: the organizational structure, the timetable, the way the rooms are arranged.'

A flexible curriculum   Organizing the curriculum in a modular approach can increase the interest and motivation in learning. In one school, for example, the science curriculum was organized into three-week 'units' each with clear objectives leading to an end-of-unit test at different levels. This allows the vast majority of pupils to be capable of achieving at least foundation level. 'Pupils have found this very motivating because of the clear objectives that they can aim at.'

The learning school seeks to arrange the learning process in such a way that it is flexible enough to meet the needs of all within the community: for example, by constructing modular courses that allow accumulation of credit or by developing open or distance learning programmes in the community. It seeks to break down the barriers between formal and informal learning, so as to positively reinforce the achievement of the learner.

A developmental curriculum   Ensuring that the learning process builds upon previous knowledge and understanding so as to achieve continuity and progression is an essential task for schools: 'We believe

that our education system should provide a planned continuity of
learning for children and young people'. Continuity should exist
between years and between stages of education. Particularly important phases of transition are between primary and secondary and in
the education of 16- to 19-year-olds which requires close collaboration between schools and colleges.

Continuity and progression are also important aspects of the
curriculum as it is taught in the classroom. A curriculum develops
not only across phases, but also within particular 'units' and lessons
and, crucially, within particular interactions between the teacher
and the students. Here an adviser discusses progression in terms of
meeting the particular needs of each young person:

> You try to get a clear idea of what a child can do, in order to
> make sensible guesses about what they might do. That's all part
> of the way a good teacher programmes the child's learning.
> You're always taking things forward. So, it's not just a matter
> of measuring ability, but of understanding a child's needs. Let
> me give you a very practical example. Say I go into a classroom
> and see a couple of children just colouring in some work sheets,
> while the rest of the class are involved in independent writing.
> And I ask, 'Why are those two just colouring in?' The teacher
> says, 'Well, they can't write on their own yet.' 'Yes, but why
> are they colouring in?' 'Well, they're doing that because they
> can do it!' You see the problem is that this teacher is thinking
> about differentiation in terms of what the child can already do.
> But differentiation really ought to be on the basis of what –
> educationally speaking – the child needs. In this case those two
> children badly need to be able to write independently or they'll
> drop farther and farther behind. Colouring in work sheets isn't
> meeting their educational needs in any way. It isn't helping
> them progress.

Distinguishing students in terms of what they can already do
ensures that those who are perceived as less able remain so. Conceived in this way, differentiation can only compound the problems
of the disadvantaged student. The alternative approach advocated
by this adviser is to differentiate in terms of what students cannot
as yet do, but need to be able to do. This requires meticulous
attention to the processes of learning and to the ways in which
students can be helped to move forward in their learning. 'You
always have chances,' as one teacher put it, 'you never run out
of chances. There's always another chance, a way through.' What

the learning school offers are opportunities for students to go on learning and teachers who are committed to helping their students find 'a way through'.

Positive assessment

If students are to make progress in learning, their work and achievement must be monitored and reviewed. Assessing achievement is regarded properly as a positive process which seeks to encourage students by recognizing their achievements and thus reinforcing their motivation. That process places a strong emphasis on:

Recording and celebrating achievement   Achievement is the prime focus of formative assessment: 'We need to commend and celebrate children's achievement. Even to say "well done" costs little but means so much. It reinforces motivation to learn.' Another teacher emphasized the importance of visual display as a means of recognizing achievement and of making that recognition public: 'How often does an individual pupil have work on display in the school? What steps have been taken to display pupils' work further afield?' In many schools students' achievements are regularly communicated to parents and given public acknowledgement in house or year assemblies: 'What matters is that we create a climate of success and that we take a pride in one another's achievements'. Achievement is the result of focused effort and, in their commitment to acknowledge it, teachers are recognizing the capacity of their students to progress and develop.

Caring and supportive relationships   Teachers must develop a detailed knowledge of their students based upon a caring relationship so that they can make informed judgements about the education that will be appropriate to their needs: 'More than anything, the words are important – and the relationships. All the other things in a sense come later.' Careful assessment allows teachers and students to diagnose strengths and weaknesses and to identify and plan how improvements can be made in the future. This can involve teachers and students negotiating and committing themselves to improving achievement: 'What opportunities are pupils given to assess their own educational progress? What system exists for taking into account pupils' or parents' suggestions for future activities?' Part of the process of empowering students is to support them, through ongoing dialogue, in their own development as learners: 'You have to make sure that assessment doesn't just mean entering ticks against a long list of attainment targets. What it must do is involve teachers in talking with children about their learning, giving them positive feedback about their work and, above all, valuing what they say. It's about maintaining the dialogue.'

Student self-assessment and peer review   If assessment is to be effective for the student it must involve an element of self-assessment. Some teachers spoke of how assessment is a shared endeavour: 'Whenever I assess a piece of work now I always ask the student about it. Did they enjoy doing it? Was it too easy or too hard? Are they pleased with it? Only then do I make my comments.' This process of self-assessment may lead to students talking about their work together: 'I try to leave time for them to read one another's work and discuss their responses. I'm sure they learn more that way than if I was just giving it a mark out of ten'. Students working together to understand how they might improve and develop is central to a formative and positive approach to assessment.

Close liaison between teachers   Positive assessment requires close liaison between pastoral and curriculum aspects of schooling. In many schools the distinction between pastoral and academic responsibilities is being rethought with a view to tutors and subject teachers working more closely together in support of learning. While the tutor can provide a vital overview of student progress across subjects, only the subject teacher can engage in a detailed discussion of the student's progress within that subject. This means that the subject teacher is required to talk with students on a one-to-one basis about their learning and about any problems they may be encountering in relation to their work. The tutor augments that ongoing dialogue between teachers and students and on occasion may be asked to mediate or offer an alternative perspective. But the role of the subject teacher in maintaining and pushing forward the dialogue is central.

To be effective, however, the liaison needs to operate across as well as within schools. One adviser outlined the systems that had been set in place within his particular LEA: 'These include standardized tests designed to identify the kind of help and support individual children need in primary school. It has also developed graded tests and statements of achievement in secondary schools, which record how far a pupil has mastered a set of skills or a piece of learning. The purpose of these tests is not to distinguish between pupils or to select the most able; their role is to encourage by giving recognition to each pupil's level of achievement.' Teachers from different schools sometimes meet in subject groups to check and validate standards of pupil achievement.

> Teachers have found the process of monitoring standards very supportive. They have gathered in 'cluster meetings' of three or four schools. They have taken samples of their pupils' work and argued through how that particular bit of work matches various criteria and statements until they achieve a consensus ... It is supportive for teachers because they know they are doing the right thing and they know comparable work is going on in other schools ... If they find a problem with a unit there is an immediate mechanism for feeding this back in to the centre.

Integrating learning and assessment   Excellent systems of assessment are integral to the process of improving the quality of learning. Within the classroom the teacher's professional role is to monitor closely the progress made by each student, negotiating work with students to ensure a proper level of expectations: 'You raise aspirations by setting achievable tasks, and setting targets which expect them to improve':

> Students can underachieve if teachers become complacent in this. But if a whole course is set up so that tasks are available and it is quite clear which tasks the students are going to move on to and when the task is completed it is brought back to the member of staff for checking and then there is negotiation for the students to move on to the next stage. I think using this method students are far more likely to keep or to increase their motivation ... but monitoring is the key: record-keeping and monitoring has got to be absolutely superb.

This emphasis on teachers negotiating with students about their own learning has important implications for how teachers manage their classrooms and how they see their own role within the classroom: 'It has to do with how you see yourself, whether you see yourself as a giver of knowledge, or a facilitator of learning, or as the provider of an environment in which learning can take place.' Another teacher spoke of the demands it makes on teachers in terms of the need for flexibility and variety of approach: 'If you're into just standing at the front of the classroom all the time and talking at children as opposed to with them, then you're going to find it very hard.'

Codes of cognitive differentiation

The values and practices celebrated in the previous two sections of this chapter have developed against an overall conception of learning that we have characterized as 'selective differentiation' (see Chapter 2). The underlying assumption of that particular conception is that schools differentiate in order to select students for their particular places within the socio-economic order. Throughout the post-war era that process of selective differentiation has been carried forward by a variety of practices: the provision of different schools for students judged at 11+ to be of different abilities; the streaming of students according to ability within a single institution; the provision of alternative curricula for those with special educational needs; and, most recently, the development of standard testing procedures for all students at 7, 11, 14 and 16.

The learning school sets itself against these developments: while seriously concerned with recognizing individual difference, it is also deeply committed to equality and eschews any form of social, cultural or intellectual selection. Its concern with differentiation, therefore, is based on very different assumptions than those which underpin the selective tradition. Within the learning school, differentiation becomes the site of an historic struggle over educational ends and purposes. That struggle – a clash of codes – is crucial to our understanding of the values and practices outlined above.

Contrasting approaches to differentiation

Simpson and Ure (1993), in a recent study of differentiation in Scottish secondary schools, describe the values and practices of differentiation on three different dimensions, according to the extent to which the 'locus of differentiation' rests in:

> *the pupil* – his or her placement on a workscheme, in a group or in a class, according to some perceived set of characteristics or level of attainment;
> *the course materials* – which differ in level of difficulty or other characteristics;
> *the activity of the teacher* – the use of the face-to-face encounter with pupils to make a spontaneous response, which is differentiated according to a complex and ever-changing set of perceptions of their differences.
>
> (p.11)

The first two dimensions are associated with an identifiable approach to classroom management. Where the 'loci of differentiation' are the placing and setting of students and the use of differentiated materials, good practice is likely to be seen as 'highly structured and largely based on individualised learning schemes on which pupils were placed according to their individual attainments on end-of-unit criterion referenced tests, and according to their individual rates of progress' (p.52). The mode of learning is likely to be highly individualized: that of 'a relatively solitary individual learner interacting with a text which has been selected on the basis of that learner's previous history of attainment under those same conditions of learning' (p.52). Relationships between teacher and students are likely to be heavily framed, with the role of the teacher tending towards a limited number of prespecified functions and offering little opportunity for spontaneous interaction. This model of differentiation, argue Simpson and Ure, is 'regarded by many secondary teachers as the epitome of differentiation – a pre-structured curriculum, with different routes being selected for different pupils on the basis of their different competencies' (p.52).

The third dimension represents an alternative approach to differentiation, 'characterised by the high level of face-to-face interaction between teachers and pupils' (p.53). In classrooms where this approach is practised, 'a subtle and complex pedagogy had evolved, which many of the teachers themselves did not regard as differentiation, but which nevertheless provided educational experiences which were accurately matched to the separate requirements of a diverse group of pupils' (p.86). Typically, time would be devoted to 'class, group and individual exchanges with the teacher, allowing the latter ample opportunity for the diagnosis of curricular, cognitive or personal difficulties, as well as for an evaluation of the effectiveness of the teaching strategy adopted with particular individuals' (p.28). A wide variety of appropriate texts and stimuli would be offered to all students, with differentiation being achieved 'by task' and 'by outcome', rather than 'by input'. Learning thereby becomes a two-way process, with students giving and receiving information and teachers listening as well as telling: 'in the classrooms in which this type of differentiation was most in evidence, a warm personal rapport between the teacher and the class had been established, in the context of which, individual and targeted feedback was given to pupils' (p.29).

Students themselves, Simpson and Ure found, had a view of themselves as learners which more closely corresponded with this second approach. Data from pupil interviews they conducted indicated

that students consider they learn better when they have a good
relationship with the teacher; when the fact of their having difficulties is noticed by the teacher; when they are given appropriate
support to resolve their difficulties; when the teacher offers useful
explanations and ensures that these explanations are understood;
and when they are given speedy and effective feedback on their
progress (p.76). Students were quite clear that what helped them to
learn

> was not an individualised scheme or set of resources, not a
> particular form of grouping or set of activities, but a *teacher* –
> a teacher who was readily available and approachable, who
> noticed when they had difficulties, who took time and trouble
> to give them explanations which they were able to understand,
> who paced the work appropriately, who set realistic goals for
> them in the short and long term, and who gave them good
> quality and timely feedback on their performance.
>
> (p.78)

Weston and Barrett (1992), who conducted a study of curriculum coherence and whole-school management in English secondary schools, have noted a recurrent ambivalence among secondary
school teachers towards the practices associated with differentiation. Although none of the case study schools that formed part of
the study had introduced setting or streaming, the reorganization of
student groups was a live issue: 'All the schools were worried about
the future of mixed-ability teaching groups. Many teachers suggested
that, even with an efficient pupil record system, they would not
be able to differentiate the curriculum to ensure curriculum progression for every child in large, mixed-ability groups' (p.158). The
influence of GCSE policy and practice could be felt strongly, with
the phrase 'differentiation by input' being associated, for some
teachers, with the allocation of students 'to different papers, largely
different courses and, in many cases, different teaching groups'
(p.159). Perhaps because of these uncertainties Weston and Barrett
found little evidence of schools prioritizing a whole-school policy
on differentiation.

Underlying assumptions

The lesson for school management that we would want to draw
from these studies and from our own analyses is that differentiation
is not simply a matter of doing different things with different pupils.
It also poses important questions about the quality of the relation-

ships within the classroom: relationships between students and between students and teachers. As such it raises issues regarding the deep underlying assumptions, or codes, of classroom practice. It is to these underlying assumptions that we must look in order to make sense of differentiation as currently practised.

The various practices of differentiation are highly coded and rest upon assumptions which are rarely made explicit, but which determine how and why they are used:

Assumptions about the nature of knowledge   Highly structured systems of differentiation, whether by student placement or by course material, often rest on the assumption that the knowledge within a particular subject is hierarchically ordered and that competence in that subject is therefore gained serially. Learning is seen as an ordered progression through a hierarchy of knowledge and skill mediated by the stable competence of the individual student. Differentiation that relies upon face-to-face interaction and dialogue between student and teacher questions, at least by implication, that assumption. It embodies a view of cognition as inherently unpredictable in its outcomes and highly variable in its processes.

Assumptions about student capacity and capability   An assumption underpinning many of the practices associated with differentiation is that what a student can realistically be expected to achieve in the future is determined by a set of stable and unalterable characteristics which are often categorized as 'general ability'. Each student, in other words, has certain capabilities that match her or his predetermined capacity. A dialogical approach to differentiation, on the other hand, would question whether the outcomes of learning can be predicted in this way. It equates individuality with potentiality and sees the role of the teacher as being to ensure that learning is a process whereby we become ourselves.

Assumptions about the learning process   Differentiation may be premised on the further assumption that learning is a relatively solitary activity in which the learner interacts with a text, or a task, that has been selected on the basis of that learner's previous history of attainment. Although nominally a member of the teaching group, the student is involved in a process which sets her or him apart. The alternative approach is to equate differentiation with the inherently social process of individuation: a process whereby individual students progress through interaction and dialogue.

Assumptions about the role of the teacher   Differentiation conceived solely in terms of student placement or course materials carries with it an assumption that the teacher controls the mechanisms and systems of learning. The teacher is always at one remove, managing the resources of the classroom in addition to the assessment procedures, with the risk that little or no personal feedback is given to students during a lesson and that the assessments carried out at the end of each unit are not used formatively or diagnostically, but simply as a further means of assigning students to different levels. Differentiation by dialogue challenges this assumption and views learning as a deeply collaborative endeavour.

Assumptions about the function of schools Many of the practices associated with differentiation seem still to be a part of a selective tradition based upon a view of the school as a prime site of social stratification. Those practices sort students, place them and locate them according to their supposed capabilities and, in spite of the expansion and diversification of higher education, effectively place a ceiling on their educational opportunities. Differentiation may also, however, through its emphasis on the capacity of each student for progress and development, set itself against that selective tradition. It can open up opportunities for individual students and help define the function of the school in terms of the agency and capacity of its learners.

Equality of difference: towards a conception of integrative differentiation

A support teacher in English and humanities spoke eloquently of what we would see as some of the more positive aspects of differentiation as currently practised:

> Effective teaching is central to countering underachievement. Teaching method is now the key issue. Mixed-ability – or as I prefer to call it, 'mixed-need' teaching is essential to avoid streaming and selection within schools. Even the idea of mixed 'ability' presupposes that we can grade, select and differentiate young people. The emphasis is then upon difference between pupils in a way that organizes and reinforces inequality within schools.
>
> Yet children have different needs and require different work. What then becomes important is the organization and ethos of the class in order to allow both social cohesion and an opportunity for each child to be successful. There has in the past been a collusion in mediocrity between teachers and pupils: teachers agree not to push and stretch children in exchange for a cosy atmosphere. The need is to develop new strategies that

encourage more classroom talk, personal writing, active learning strategies.

In mixed-need teaching the aim is to make sure that each
child's needs are catered for, but this includes working in groups
and sharing activities, not just a separate education for each
child. A key theme is variety so that pupils are involved in
different kinds of lesson . . .

This strategy of mixed-need teaching involves a shift in philosophy and practice for teachers. It is difficult. It means more
work for teachers: more preparation, extra homework, marking, giving children feedback. These are simple expectations of
teachers but they put them under pressure.

This emphasis on 'mixed-need teaching' – on group work, sharing
and a variety of teaching styles – points to the dual emphasis in much
current educational practice on the recognition of difference *and* on
the importance of equalizing opportunities. It is that dual emphasis
that enables the learning school to challenge the traditional conception of learning as 'selective differentiation' and to reconceptualize
it as a process of differentiation whereby individuals realize their
full capacities and powers. Learning so conceived is a deeply integrative process in that it unites the self and enables it to achieve
agency through interaction with others and through engagement
with the world. The learning school seeks to encourage this process
through an increased emphasis on:

Learning as participation   Learning requires co-operation and collaboration and continually reaches out into the public domain. Learning confirms our sense of membership within the various contexts
and communities of life.

Learning as dialogue   Learning is active and interactive and necessarily involves a recognition of – and exploration of – the other.
Learning confirms our sense of self through the experience of
engaging with other people's ideas and feelings.

Learning as partnership   Learning is achieved across complex, interlocking boundaries of institutional and cultural life. Learning confirms the need for shared understanding across those boundaries
and for a recognition of the rich resources of our communities.

Learning as life-long   Learning is a process that continues throughout our lives, enabling us to extend our horizons and shape our life
histories. Learning is what, in prospect, makes of life a quest and
what, in retrospect, makes of it a narrative.

FOUR

The learning school II

Learning, we have argued, is structured by institutional and cultural codes that both generate and constrain social practice. Initially, the learner may be unaware of the influence of these codes. However, if learning is to develop and deepen, that influence must be acknowledged and challenged. Learning progresses as learners question what they had previously taken for granted or assumed to be part of the natural order of things. That is why we have conceptualized learning in terms of a number of interdependent layers: through learning we not only define and make ourselves, but do so by participating in the creation of a world in which, inescapably, we live together. The bases of learning are at once individual, interpersonal *and* public.

Most organizations, however, tend to atomize the social and personal processes that constitute learning, adopting a working definition of learning that cuts learning off from its institutional and cultural roots. Schools are no exception. As we argued in Chapter 2, their underlying codes have traditionally generated practices that tend towards exclusivity: hierarchy in terms of staff and student participation, specialization in terms of the dominant modes of professionalism and closure in terms of boundary management. They have tended, that is, to reflect in their organizational and management practices a tradition of selective differentiation that has been dominant in the practices of curriculum, pedagogy and assessment; a tradition that manages difference by organizing it into systems of inequality. The management of difference remains, therefore, our central theme as we shift the level of our exposition to focus upon the internal organization of the learning school.

The educational challenge, we argue, is to reintegrate the social and personal processes of learning so as to ensure long-term commitment to purposeful change based upon equality of difference. In this chapter we show how that task of reintegration involves schools in shifting the assumptions that underlie their organizational practices and, in particular, those practices that relate to their relation to their public. As in the previous chapter, we perceive significant shifts at a number of levels:

- value-driven institutional development
- integrative practice:
  collegiality: dialogue and deliberation
  collaboration: institutions working together
  partnership: schools, parents and their public
- codes of cultural differentiation.

Value-driven institutional development

The values which drive the institutional practices and organizational structures of the learning school are centrally concerned with participation and involvement, with the continual search for quality and with public accountability. The learning school values:

Vision and purpose Learning schools, although often situated in areas of extreme disadvantage, never give up on their students and offer their communities hope for the future: 'Where schools really go down the plug, the drain, whatever the phrase is, people have lost hope and a sense that they can improve: it becomes hopeless . . . Very, very, very few schools are failing schools'. It offers a vision of learning and of support for learning: 'What we need to do is to refocus and put learning at the centre of everything that we do'. Leadership is about building a sense of institutional identity around a shared sense of purpose: 'My prime task', as one head teacher put it, 'is to make sure that we all agree on fundamental principles, like where we are heading and why.' Another recently appointed head also acknowledged the importance of working 'through the staff': 'I have come in with a very clear view in my mind in terms of what I want to do as far as raising standards, if you like, in terms of academic achievement and ambition and self-esteem and vision for young people, and I have got to do that through the staff.' The idea of the school as a community of learners sharing a common purpose is central to the institutional development of the learning school.

Staff involvement Collaboration and consultation at all levels are an essential feature of the learning school. Teachers see themselves as team members and curriculum development is approached as a whole-school task:

We have working parties on a number of cross-curriculum themes. Working in that kind of cross-curriculum team is important because it helps you see the curriculum as a whole. There's a danger of burrowing away and just seeing your bit. But when you're trying to see how the various bits can all contribute to equal opportunities, say, or to our overall work on citizenship, then you've got to look up and take a wider view.

The task of senior management is to ensure that everyone on the staff feels valued and that what each contributes to the life of the school is fully acknowledged: 'We ask a great deal of all our staff and I know they feel the strain, but all the hard work is acknowledged and I think just about everyone occasionally feels this great surge of fulfilment in knowing that we're really turning this school round.'

The search for quality   Institutional self-evaluation is integral to the task of curriculum and professional development. Teachers are expected to reflect upon their own and one another's practice and are given the resources to do so. 'It isn't good enough just to keep churning out the same old lessons. You have to think about your own teaching and the effect it's having on your classes. And that means talking with colleagues and being willing to change.' Quality is seen not as a commodity to be acquired and held on to, but as a process of development requiring self-reflection and continuing dialogue with colleagues: 'As a school we believe the only way to improve is to keep looking at what we are doing and to monitor that very carefully. I don't just mean looking at a few output measures every now and then, although that's an important part of it. I mean all of us looking at our own work as teachers and at the quality of the work in our classrooms and beginning to talk with one another about it.'

Accountability to the public   The learning school sees itself as offering a public service to the local community and recognizes that it is accountable for the quality of service it provides. It is highly sceptical of the crude measures of comparability currently used to differentiate between schools in vastly different areas and seeks to attune its accountability procedures to the needs of the particular publics it serves. This means an increased emphasis on public dialogue as to what constitutes quality in education: 'It's important that people understand what, as a school, we are trying to do – otherwise we could be judged by all the wrong standards. Judgements about education are often so glib. Any helpful judgement about this school would have to be based on a real knowledge of where we are and where we are going'. Genuine accountability calls not only the school to account, but the communities the school serves and the families which form those communities: 'We're in this together. We really are. If it's going to work, it can't just be schools on their own. It's got to be all of us.'

Parent participation Parents play a central role in the education of their children. Within the learning school they are valued as complementary educators and encouraged to participate fully in the education of their children. Schools emphasize the importance of parents being involved in and understanding the learning process: 'We believe it is very important to work alongside parents, keeping them informed about the progress of their child and involving them as much as possible in the life of the school'. Parents are respected as having the best interests of their children at heart: 'It's easy to say that we're going to have a hard task just because the parents at this school are working class. But that's not necessarily the case. There are lots of working-class parents here who have very high expectations for their children. Expectations are rising all the time and they're rising among working-class parents as well. They want the very best for their children.' Parents are also seen as having something important and unique to bring to the learning process: 'Their experience is so important and diverse – we need to draw on it and help parents to see how important they really are for the education of their own children.' Without that involvement many schools believe their task is an impossible one: 'Parental support is just so important. Without it I believe we are almost bound to fail. But if parents back us and work with us, then we're in with a real chance.'

Community involvement 'The idea needs to be fostered that a school cannot exist without serving the community'. Both the school and the community benefit when each works with the other: 'All schools should work interactively with the local neighbourhood and the wider community. The relationship of a school with the community it serves is vital both to the educational process and to the well-being of that community. Schools should be prime resources which facilitate learning for all, in partnership with other providers, [and] in which the curriculum relates to and reflects the needs of its community.' The learning school is committed to improving the quality of life in the community, enabling self-confidence and celebrating achievement so as to reinforce the motivation and ability

of all: 'Community education can offer people a sense of achievement by enabling them to make a wider contribution to their community . . . This also provides people with a sense of purpose and
meaning in their lives. Achievement can lead to positive feedback,
strengthening self-image and confidence'. Underlying this perspective
is the belief that community involvement is a precondition for the
regeneration of highly disadvantaged communities: 'It will improve
the quality of life: involving the community will improve the confidence, performance and effectiveness of the community and its
individuals'.

Integrative practice

The learning school is characterized by collegial, collaborative and
partnership practices which express the values outlined in the previous section. These practices seek to integrate the organizational
structures of schooling through systems of *dialogue and deliberation*
which involve the whole staff and require participation and commitment; *institutions working together* in such a way as to provide a
coherent and continuous public education service; and *schools, parents and the public* working together in partnership.

Dialogue and deliberation

Good schools take seriously the need to increase the level of participation by all staff in decision-making regarding every aspect of
school life. Professional relationships are collegial: shaped by shared
values and tasks, not by hierarchies of status and esteem. Teachers
are seen as learners, who – like their students – are developing and
in need of support and encouragement. The internal organization
and ethos of the learning school emphasize:

Cross-curriculum planning Planning is seen as a cross-curricular activity, involving teachers from different subject areas working together
to achieve curriculum coherence and continuity. Many schools have
now established cross-curriculum working parties in some or all of
the cross-curriculum themes and dimensions: 'The working party
on economic and industrial understanding meets regularly and brings
together representatives from almost every department in the school.
We have conducted a curriculum audit to see how the theme is
currently distributed . . . and we're now in a position to plug the
gaps and build on our strengths. We also draw on the experience of

local industry and business as and when appropriate'. In another school the prime focus of cross-curriculum planning is citizenship education:

> It started with a group of teachers mainly from the humanities subjects, but now also includes colleagues from science, maths and the performing arts. What we've tried to do is define an entitlement for children around what they need to know about their own rights and about their responsibilities towards others. We're not planning actual lessons – that's up to the departments themselves – but we are offering guidelines and suggestions that we hope department teams will pick up on.

Increasingly the traditional divide between pastoral and academic staff is dissolving, with tutors and heads of house or year playing a central role in cross-curriculum planning and in the recording and assessment procedures that accompany it: 'We're much more curriculum-led than we used to be. That doesn't mean that we don't care for our students. It means that we try to focus our care on their individual learning needs. The pastoral and the academic are really just different ways of looking at the same thing and that's reflected in the way we work together and plan our programmes of work.' In many schools cross-curriculum planning is organized around work experience or other off-site experiences that provide an opportunity for interdisciplinary enquiry:

> We try to build into the curriculum learning experiences that take the children out of school and that we can follow up in different subjects. Often a single department will take prime responsibility for organizing the particular off-site programme, but in consultation with teachers from other departments, who then use the student's experience in their own lessons. It takes a lot of planning and consultation, but it's worth it in terms of what the children get out of it.

Whole-school policy development The development of whole-school policies on issues that are of concern to all teachers and students provides a further opportunity for dialogue and deliberation. Typically, such policies would cover issues relating to multiculturalism and anti-racism, gender and equal opportunities for boys and girls, discipline and the quality of relationships in and around the school. In developing policies in these areas, schools see the process of policy development being as important as the final product: 'The policy in itself is of little value unless it has the agreement and backing of the school as a whole. So the process whereby the statement is arrived at is immensely important. In agreeing our equal opportunities policy we involved not only the whole staff, but also students and parents in the consultation procedure. It took a long time but now we are all behind it. It's much more than just a token document. We really live and work by it.' At the same time, however, the statement itself has symbolic value and transmits a powerful message to staff, students and parents: 'It's a way of declaring what we're about and what we stand for.'

School policy statements cannot be set in tablets of stone and require regular renegotiation and redrafting if they are to represent fairly and fully the values and commitments of the school: 'We changed our discipline policy statement quite radically when we decided we had got to take bullying seriously as a problem that affects many of our students'. In another school the multicultural policy was being revised to take greater cognizance both of changing patterns of cultural diversity within the school and of the staff's growing awareness of the extent and complexity of that diversity:

> We used to think multicultural education was something to do with the fact that 10 per cent of our young people are black. Well, of course, that's partly true, but only partly. There's great diversity within that 10 per cent and we also have Irish children, children from Eastern Europe, and also there's great diversity within what you might describe as the indigenous white population. It's much more complicated than we thought and we're trying to recognize that complexity in revising the policy statement.

Working in teams   The experience of team membership is central to the experience of working in a learning school: 'If you ask me who leads this school I'd have to say it's the teams. They're terribly important to our way of working – department teams, year teams, various liaison teams, the senior management team . . . Most members of staff are members of more than one team, depending on what responsibilities they're assuming at the time. It's the teams that drive us and move us on.' Working in this way teachers feel they learn from one another and that any curriculum change that is brought about is likely to be more enduring and more likely to be accepted by the staff as a whole: 'It doesn't matter how innovative you are, if you're just burrowing away on your own it's not going to have any impact. You've got to work with your colleagues and take them with you.'

Schools offering residential experience to students find that, while making important demands on the students themselves, it also demands intensive team work from teachers who may not routinely work together: 'It raised fundamental issues about how we work together and who does what. Who drives the minibus for example? Who takes on the disciplinary role and who calms things down? Who thinks it might be a good idea to nip down to the pub when the kids are finally in bed? No equal opportunities workshop could possibly have raised our awareness as successfully as that four days away'. The experience of working in teams changes the nature of many of the problems that teachers have to face. It demands a much greater level of collegial accountability, but means that teachers are less isolated professionally and that decisions are more likely to be made collectively or at least with reference to collectively defined values and priorities. The experience can be unnerving, but is invariably transforming: 'Sometimes I almost resent having to explain myself to colleagues. Why can't I just get on with it and do my own thing? But then I tell myself that I'm actually in a much stronger position. I'm not just acting on my own. It's a very different way of thinking about teaching.'

Support for professional development   Professional development is seen as integral to the school's practices and as the responsibility not just of the individual teacher but of the school as a whole. Teachers emphasize the importance of a variety of professional development experiences through, for example, departmental meetings and workshops, links with local institutions of higher education, exhibitions and displays, the opportunity to attend conferences and seminars, work placements and shadowing. One head spoke of the importance of ensuring that professional development is seen as lifelong: 'As a teacher you're constantly developing. What I need now in terms of professional development is completely different from what I needed ten years ago or even five. That's partly because I'm changing and learning and also because the world is changing around me.'

Time is a crucial factor and many teachers claimed that they had too little time to reflect upon their own work: 'It's difficult to grow and develop when you feel that every minute of every day is already accounted for.' Schools are trying to tackle this problem of overload in different ways. One head of department, for example, spoke of the importance of creating a climate where teachers can talk about their teaching and about the problems they may be facing:

I've worked in schools where it was considered some kind of breach of professional ethics to talk shop in the staff room. Well, I know we all need time out, but if we can't actually take a lively interest in our own teaching, what are we doing here? That's my view, anyway, and I try to build that into our work as a department. We have a department room where we have coffee together and where it's considered all right to talk about teaching. I want people just to feel free to share their problems and ideas. We try to support one another.

Teachers also spoke, however, of the value of meeting with teachers from other institutions, as well as with other professionals, and of the importance of schools supporting teachers who wished to attend external meetings, seminars and conferences: 'I feel I need to widen my horizons every now and then; meet people with different problems, different ideas.'

A school-wide system for evaluation and review The learning school approaches evaluation as a whole-school, internally generated endeavour, not just as a top-down exercise in accountability. Evaluation involves everyone, staff and students, and is ongoing: 'We're constantly gathering feedback – from one another and from the students – and we use this in the day-to-day planning and revising of our courses.' A number of schools use paired or team teaching as a means of stimulating and informing staff debate regarding the effectiveness of particular teaching methods and the quality of the learning experience: 'We organize the timetable in such a way that it's fairly easy within a particular curriculum area to combine teaching groups and allow teachers to work together in the classroom. This may mean little more than two teachers coming together to share a common resource – say, a video. But it can also provide an opportunity for teachers to observe one another's teaching and the way in which each relates to the children.'

Information that is routinely gathered as part of the school's monitoring and review procedures is fed back to staff for analysis and discussion. This includes information on attendance and student performance: 'There's no point in collecting information for the sake of it or, more likely, because someone has told you to. That's just dead information. All the information we collect is used. It's pushed back to staff through various meetings and works its way into a complex process of analysis that we take very seriously.' Such a process helps ensure that evaluation is seen as a means of illuminating the values that drive the school's practice: 'It's not a matter of saying that lesson worked and that one didn't. It's not about grading or ranking. It's about improvement – improving your own practice by understanding. I happen to think that it's very important for people to respect one another. So I have to ask myself how my own teaching is helping them or hindering them from doing that. I have to understand what's happening in my classroom in relation to my own principles.'

Institutions working together

Currently, there is great pressure on schools to compete against each other for students, particularly for bright students. Yet many schools are resisting this trend and insisting on the need for a close working relationship with other primary and secondary schools in the neighbourhood as well as with institutions of further and higher education. The learning school works towards closer collaborative ties with other institutions through:

Primary/secondary liaison   The transfer of information regarding individual students and their progress is an essential aspect of ensuring continuity across the phases and is common practice in most schools. Some schools, however, have gone beyond this formal requirement and are developing close, collaborative links across the primary/secondary divide. One school, for example, is involved in a scheme whereby, once a fortnight, the English, mathematics, science and special needs departments each sends a teacher to one of the five main primary feeder schools for two hours to talk with, and work alongside, the primary staff: 'We felt we wanted to work very closely with our primary colleagues so as to ease the transition from primary to secondary . . . We need to know how well our children are doing at primary school – and in what ways they are doing well – so that we can continue to encourage them when they come here. They need to see the continuity for themselves.' This means that prior to transfer, all students with learning difficulties have met, and in some cases begun to work with, a teacher from the special needs department. It also means that English, mathematics and science teachers have met and taught a significant proportion of students in their final year of primary school and that equipment and resources from the secondary school have been used by teachers and students within the primary classroom. The result, as one of the secondary teachers involved in the scheme put it, is that 'the links we have got with the primary staff are tremendous and the benefits to the students enormous'.

Some primary schools also involve students in developing profiles of themselves that they can use to introduce themselves to their new form teacher in the secondary school and also to other students within their new school. One teacher described these profiles as 'where I am – this is me' statements that could include various pieces of work together with the student's own thoughts about moving from primary to secondary school: 'It's a way of helping them prepare for what will be a big change in their lives – a way of getting it in perspective.' From the secondary school's point of view, such a profile can also constitute a useful springboard into the more formal processes of recording achievement.

In certain areas, 'pyramids' of schools, comprising secondary schools and their feeder primaries, have established groups which meet on a regular basis to review common concerns. A secondary head who is attached to such a group explained how the strength of collegial relationships within the 'cluster' is one of the means by which the schools are able to withstand the more destructive effects of the market:

> One of the main aims that we all share is to maintain as far as possible the comprehensive intake of this school. We would all hate to see brighter, more aspiring students drift away to other schools. So our continuing relationship – as institutions and as professionals – is absolutely vital. All the primary heads without exception are with us on this one. The (cross-school) committee is doing an important job – but it is only one aspect of an organic process that is rooted in real collaboration at the classroom level.

Collaborative curriculum development   In many areas one of the most significant legacies of the TVEI extension has been the development of 'clusters' of schools. Originally the clusters were a mechanism for bringing together the TVEI school and college co-ordinators for the purposes of curriculum development and review. Regular meetings would be held and additional staff asked to come along as and when appropriate. However, many of the clusters have taken on a life of their own and now survive outside the TVEI framework. They provide an opportunity for sharing ideas, developing materials and exploring common issues and concerns across institutions. One cluster, for example, developed a programme of work on equal opportunities for use in tutorial groups and in PSE classes: 'Because we were bringing together people from a number of schools we were able to draw on a much wider range of expertise and resources. We've developed what I think is a very important resource that we'll be able to update and, hopefully, use for several years in the future.' Another cluster worked on a profiling system for use across the schools and colleges in the region: 'Working together in that way is very important. You're not just producing a document, you're also sharing information about the different contexts in which it will be used. You're sharing ideas and agreeing a way of working.'

In other areas teachers have been encouraged to work together through the support offered by their own professional organizations, many of which have local and regional branches, or by externally funded curriculum development projects. For example, the School Curriculum Industry Partnership (SCIP) has provided regional co-ordinators and regional and national networks that continue to bring together groups of teachers with a shared interest in drawing on the resources of the local industrial community: 'It's given me an opportunity to meet with other teachers in the area and to attend national conferences. I always know that I can pick up the phone and talk to someone on the network who will try and help or be willing to listen. It's been a lifeline.' Such networks have proved particularly important given the severe contraction of LEA advisory services, which in the past many teachers have looked to for in-service support and development.

Cross-school evaluation Evaluation has become so closely associated with the external inspection of individual institutions that it is difficult to see how schools would readily work together on evaluative tasks. Yet they do, and the reason is that many teachers see evaluation not as a ranking exercise but as a means of developing and sharing their understanding of the processes of teaching and learning. One group of schools, for example, set out to evaluate its own practice in the light of a shared commitment to equal opportunities: 'We prepared for the evaluation over about a term and then spent half a term reviewing one another's curriculum materials and sitting in on one another's lessons. Then we got together over the next half term to talk it all through. It was incredibly helpful and we all feel much more confident about our own classroom practice as a result.' In other areas teachers come together to review their work within a particular curriculum area: 'It started with two of us and has just grown. We meet about twice a term and each time focus on a particular topic. Last time we met about seven people turned up and one of the group told us about a course of lessons she had prepared for a particularly difficult Year 9 class she has got. We talked it through and people shared their own experiences and ideas.'

Linking with institutions of further and higher education   Schools need to establish firm links with neighbouring institutions of further and higher education so as to ensure curriculum continuity post-16. Visits from colleagues working in the further and higher education sectors are one way in which this is achieved: 'Our kids tend to think that anybody teaching in a college is from a different planet. If they can actually talk to some of these people it helps them see that they're human.' A number of schools organize joint schemes with institutions of higher education whereby older students are given the opportunity of residential experience in a higher educa-tion setting: 'Most of our young people have never known anyone – other than the odd teacher – who has been to a university. It's just a different world. So to spend a weekend there is, just, amaz-ing. It's like you or me being catapulted up to Mars!'. Another teacher spoke of the importance of meeting with colleagues in further and higher education: 'There's a group of us who meet together once or twice a term from the local college and university. It helps to know what they are going through . . . what they expect from their students.'

Schools, parents and the public

The learning school is a caring and welcoming school where par-ents and other members of the community are seen as positive partners. Partnership with parents is the key to improving student motivation and achievement, while service to – and involvement of – the public reflects the school's broader responsibility to pro-mote education within the community: 'We need to give more time to developing the links with parents and the community. Though we do promote the international flavour of the school and its posit-ive value for us: the various communities are involved in the life of the school, in curriculum evenings, and in religious education. It's been very beneficial. The children in turn go out into the community as part of their learning.'

The central importance of the partnership between schools, par-ents and their public is reflected in particular practices:

Relating to individual parents   The notion of a single 'parent body' sits uncomfortably with the emphasis in many schools we have visited on building strong, supportive relationships with individual parents and acknowledging that different family units have very different sets of needs. One head spoke of the importance of making parents welcome at the school and of ensuring that their diversity of backgrounds is fully acknowledged: 'Are parents made welcome by the secretary, the staff and the head? Are there signs in the community languages (and) posters which reflect the diversity of society? Are staff making the effort to speak even a few words of Urdu? Is there a parents' room? Are there surgeries for parents?'

In order to set the style of the relationship as well as to forge the ensuing partnership, some schools are developing a system of contracts, or covenants, with parents: 'Before any child joins us the parent has to have an individual interview. Here the aims are made clear and the policies are made clear and the parent has to sign a contract that they will agree with what we are about.' A teacher in another school explained how the contract is a way of making explicit joint responsibilities, so that schools and parents become partners in accountability: 'It's a way of showing parents that we take some things very seriously: like homework, attendance and behaviour. It's a statement about our responsibilities as a school and about their responsibilities as parents. It's a way of making each of us accountable to the other. And it works.'

A number of schools are finding a contract or covenant of this kind a particularly effective way of combating condoned absenteeism. Parental attitudes towards attendance represent a serious problem in many schools. Teachers spoke of parents who regularly arrange family holidays during term time and who see no contradiction between absenting their child from school in this way and their own conception of themselves as 'good' parents. 'Being a good parent', as one head teacher put it, 'means taking the family on holiday and if the only way you can afford that is by having your holiday outside the peak holiday period, well, for a lot of our parents that has to take priority.' Teachers also spoke of short-term condoned absence as an habitual occurrence within some families and of the long-term detrimental effects of this on the educational prospects of young people. In some cases, as another head teacher explained, this habit had developed through infant and junior school and been carried over as a set of parental expectations into secondary school: 'Children enter the school with a poor attitude to attendance. They were taken to their primary schools by their parents and if it was raining their parents saw no problem about waiting at home till the rain stopped. So the children started coming late. If it continued raining, as it tends to in winter, their parents thought they might as well wait till after lunch. So they start being absent for whole sessions. If it was still raining in the afternoon, they'd be absent for the whole day.'

In situations such as this a formal agreement between individual parents and the school can help to arrest a habit of poor attendance and to emphasize that learning requires certain routines and disciplines which it is the responsibility of both the school and the home to maintain. It is not just that general rules and expectations are being upheld, but that these rules and expectations are being used to strengthen and inform the school's partnership with individual parents.

Developing understanding of the learning process   Considerable effort is made by schools to involve parents in understanding new developments in the curriculum and in styles of teaching and learning. This is very often achieved through open days, or evenings, at which parents are given an opportunity to experience the curriculum at first hand:

> We are getting parents more involved in curriculum evenings . . . We run a promotion evening for third-year parents and this has a very high turn out. There was a video presentation, a talk, and then actual active learning in which the parents could go round and take part in example modules. Now that was really successful . . .
>
> I think we need to do more of this to get the parents involved and for them to see what resources are necessary. I have recently set up a learning resources technology area and we are going to have an evening for parents where they can come in and use the equipment, the desktop publisher and the interactive video, and see how the children use this equipment.
>
> So I think we have got to do more in letting the parents see what sort of learning goes on in the school in order to encourage them perhaps to contribute to the resources. And by resources I don't mean buying a computer. It's more the attitude: that the parent is prepared to have some books in the home, encourage visits, facilitate the children's own learning and research on projects.
>
> I think it is very important to encourage the parents to see that education is very wide, that they can play a part and perhaps enjoy it themselves as well.

Other schools have developed guidelines and materials to help parents support their children in particular curriculum areas and have encouraged parents to read their children's written assignments and discuss their homework tasks with them. In one school, for example, the English department has developed a system whereby student coursework assignments are commented on by both parents and teachers:

> Each half term block of work carries with it an assignment. At the beginning of each assignment parents are given information about the assignment. When the student hands it in, we ask that it be accompanied by a brief statement from the parent on a very simple form we have prepared. The teacher then reads the assignment and feeds back to both the student and the parent.
>
> It's our way of ensuring that the parent knows why we have set a particular assignment and what we feel their child needs to concentrate on in order to improve and develop. The parent's comments can often help us pinpoint a particular difficulty the student may be having and this in turn can sometimes lead to a meeting with the parent or a home visit. If parents find writing difficult – some are actually unable to write – they usually get the child to write down their comments for them. Very few parents fail to co-operate.

Parents as complementary educators in the home   The benefit of involving parents as complementary educators has long been recognized at primary and pre-school level. Traditionally, however, teachers in secondary schools have tended to cling to notions of professional autonomy and status which ill accord with the idea of parents as complementary educators. Those traditional notions are beginning to have less relevance as teachers redefine their relation to one another and to their public: 'The parent–teacher partnership should be an active one. Parents don't want to be passive recipients of what schools dole out – they want to make a contribution. The good teacher does not want a passive parent, because parents know their children best. As teachers we have to listen, to learn, to respect. There is a great mystique about the autonomy of teachers in the past.'

When parents and teachers work together, students' motivation and self-confidence increases: 'If the learning objective is improving the child's language, then the parent can listen, help with drafting, hear them read. This process shows the parent valuing the activity, reinforcing the learning process. Teachers need to extend the contribution of parents to children's learning at home . . . to think about the curriculum, the resources needed, the nature of the parental involvement. This is all part of the parent–teacher partnership.' That partnership also has a beneficial effect on student behaviour and attitudes to work: 'Discipline problems diminish radically when the partners work together. Poor behaviour and attitude problems are quickly picked up and shared. Parents sharing the personal problems helps to resolve the learning problems of the child. When you've got this you've made it.'

In a number of schools home–school visiting is seen as another important means of encouraging the parent's role as educator in the home. This may be a daunting prospect for many teachers: 'The thought of having to go into people's homes, to meet them on their own ground, causes anxiety. They are not necessarily going to meet committed people; but you have got to go in and persuade; it is possibly alien territory.' Many of the difficulties teachers have in communicating with parents – and that parents face in communicating with teachers – hark back to the parent's limited and often negative earlier experiences of schooling. Several interviewees echoed the deputy head who commented that 'many of our parents have not had happy schooling experiences themselves and school can be a daunting prospect for them'. In such cases the potential for misunderstanding between parents and teachers is immense and is likely to have long-term consequences regarding the educational achievements of the student.

Although any system of home–school visiting presents enormous resource problems for the school, it can be a highly effective means of overcoming parental fears and anxieties and of recognizing the home as an important site of learning: 'I've only managed to visit the home once, but it's made a tremendous difference. The child relates to me differently and so does the parent. We keep in contact. Since the visit she's contacted me about a particular problem . . . But the main thing is that . . . now we've got a kind of working relationship.' In some schools the development of a student record of achievement is seen to have implications for the school's relations with parents: 'We can no longer be selective, no longer say "Well, we only get some parents coming to see us but not others". Rather, we must go out to get them, to see them. It means more home visits.'

Involving parents in the learning process at school   One head spoke of a number of strategies to involve parents, including a friend's group, social events, curriculum evenings, a parental skills bank, and working closely with the governors. But it was an LEA officer for special education who was particularly articulate about the home–school partnership:

> The new school for young people with severe learning difficulties is a golden opportunity to work with parents . . . We have

built a parent's suite in the centre of the school, near to the
head's and staff rooms and to the resource facilities. This is the
first step to a philosophy which places parents at the centre as
the prime educators. Why are parents so important? . . . Teachers
may have contact with young people for 30 hours a week. But
parents have the longer-term involvement: parents are the prime
educators. Teachers have a commitment to a young person
over a period of time which then terminates: parents have the
longer-term commitment . . . There must, therefore, be the possibility of parents and teachers working together co-operatively
and collaboratively to educate the child. Parents should have
access to the education process as a right . . . I don't believe in
a parental veto. But we do need a partnership between parents
and teachers. Sometimes the school needs to act as the advoc-
ate of the child: we cannot always assume that the wants of the
parents correspond to the child's needs. They don't always.

In many mainstream schools teachers are equally insistent regarding the benefits of parental involvement and its potential impact on
the curriculum. One school, for example, emphasized cultural diversity as a prime curriculum resource: 'Asian parents can come in and
demonstrate dance, dress and food. This is not an appendage, but
a broadening and informing of the whole curriculum. It emphasizes
that the multicultural curriculum is not just about "cultures", but is
anti-racist in that children learn about the need to prevent discrimination in jobs and housing.' Another school sees its curriculum as
being enriched by the various occupational and community backgrounds of its parents.

Involving parents in designing the curriculum Schools are recognizing
that parents have an important part to play in the overall design
and development of the curriculum: 'Parental involvement in schools
– in the learning process of the child and on parent–teacher committees – is vital not just for fund-raising, but for consultation and
discussion of the curriculum: parents informing the development of
the curriculum, being involved in helping to deliver the curriculum,
in links with industry, using parents' experience of geography and
travel. If you are aware of parents' experience, this can be used to
enhance the delivery of the curriculum.' Consulting with parents
can help to inform and enrich the quality of education: it can, for
example, help 'inform and develop a multicultural and anti-racist
curriculum: parents can help teachers become aware of the images
and language they use. This is all-important for the hidden curriculum [and] needs to be planned for and communicated. Parents

have to be brought in – because it is 'a controversial issue' – to understand the objectives, what the children will gain, how it will be done.'

Partners in progress Schools are becoming increasingly concerned with keeping parents informed about how their child's learning is proceeding and about the information systems necessary for keeping them informed. One senior adviser helpfully elucidated strategies for using the National Curriculum regulations for building the partnership between teachers and parents:

> The old parents' meetings will have to go. The form teacher must have a better picture of the kids in the form, they must have better information from their colleagues. There must be an ongoing programme for teachers and individual parents to get together: once a week, say, a surgery at 4 p.m. to see one or two parents to spend a reasonable length of time going through what the pupil has done in the past period, what development plan is needed, what issues need to be addressed.

The organizational implications of such an 'ongoing programme' are awesome: 'It means a form teacher giving 30 sessions a term: say, 30 hours. There are 72 days in the next term – this is half the days available – and a conversation with parents is no good unless teachers have spoken to their colleagues.'

In spite of these problems, schools are finding ways to develop the dialogue between parents and teachers: 'You must sit down with the parents. If the child has a target of level 3 and has only reached level 2 then teachers and parents need to work out a strategy together to improve achievement. The teachers can ask what skills the parents have to offer. The whole attitude of the teacher–parent relationship has to change'. Parents need to be kept informed about progress throughout their children's school career: 'We need to examine how interest is generated. Start at the beginning: we need to find out what are the attitudes and procedures which shut parents off from their child's education (with 14- and 15-year-olds it is a lost battle). We must start from an early age. Most parents are interested, but they don't know what is going on. That is why information is so important. If they knew about the problems they would naturally get involved'.

Negotiating the curriculum with the whole community The curriculum of the learning school aspires to be a curriculum that is owned and shaped by the whole community:

What goes on in schools and the curriculum has a broader concern than just for parents of the child: it is the concern of the whole community. So our curriculum document aims to make the curriculum an open, debatable issue, not something which is shrouded in mystery. Until we have a genuinely popular education system, with a genuinely popular curriculum which ordinary people believe in and support, until you have got that you are merely pushing people through hoops which have no meaning for them.

Links with other local institutions provide an important means of negotiation: 'We have good contacts with local churches, mosques and family refuge organizations. We consult with them regularly . . . often through staff who are members of those communities'.

Codes of cultural differentiation

In this and the previous chapter we have celebrated the values and practices of what we have termed the learning school. The previous chapter explored the pedagogical, curriculum and assessment structures of schooling. This chapter has been concerned primarily with the internal organization and boundary management of the learning school and has celebrated the values and practices associated with collegiality, collaboration and partnership; values and practices that, particularly within contexts of disadvantage, have been developed in opposition to the dominant codes of hierarchy, specialization, closure and competition.

Faces of disaffection

The conditions associated with disadvantaged contexts – low standards of living, lack of control over one's own working life, job insecurity and unemployment, and the increased risk of ill-health – have a severe impact on learning. The accumulation of these conditions over time can mean that parents lack the knowledge and resources to access the education system and the confidence to make demands on it. This does not mean, however, that these parents necessarily have low expectations for their children. They may have very high expectations in the sense of wanting their children to achieve and develop. The problem is that for such parents the procedures of the school are often a closed book. This can make it difficult for them to support their children appropriately in matters of learning and adjustment; not because they are poor parents but because they lack the necessary 'cultural capital'. For their children this situation can lead to what Bernstein (1975) terms 'estrangement', whereby the student is committed to the ends and purposes of education but 'cannot manage its demands; he cannot manage the learning, he does not understand the *means*. It is all a bit too difficult for him' (p.46). If unchecked this problem can deepen into one of 'aliena-tion', whereby the student 'is positively in opposition' and relates to the school 'only in terms of conflict or sullen acceptance' (p.46).

A recurring image in many of the schools we have visited is of student disaffection at precisely that moment of transition from estrangement to alienation: the student who is not particularly rebellious, just switched off; who faces the teacher with a blank stare, a look of boredom; who no longer cares that it is all a bit too difficult. In interview, teachers have repeatedly conjured up this image in an attempt to explain their experience of student disaffec-tion. The problem as they see it lies in the restricted access to learn-ing opportunities, to life chances and to a wide range of linguistic and communicative resources. In particular they point to the lack of opportunity to acquire the routines and procedures of learning: 'We have absolutely no problem in trying to raise expectations,' as one head teacher put it, 'the problem comes when you try to get across that certain routines are necessary in order to achieve those expectations.' The students want to achieve, and their parents want them to achieve, but neither understands fully the formulae for achieving or the disciplines of study.

Lyons and Lowery (1986) have developed a conceptual model to map the behaviours and attitudes associated with disaffection in urban settings. The model builds upon the work of Hirschman (1970) and Sharp (1984a, 1984b) and has subsequently been elaborated and tested within a variety of contexts (see Lowery *et al.* 1992; Lyons and Lowery 1989; Lyons *et al.* 1992). Lyons and Lowery consider four types of participation: *exit, neglect, loyalty* and *voice* (see Figure 4.1).

Exit as an active/destructive form of response   The exit form of response involves a deliberate attempt to opt out. It includes, as typical beha-viours, truancy, refusal and disruption. Such behaviours constitute the most obvious and unavoidable face of disaffection and often place schools in an uncomfortable dilemma: either resist such beha-viours and risk greater disruption or collude with those who are behaving in that way and risk a general erosion of learning within the school. Of less damage to school and student are those instances active

VOICE	EXIT
e.g.	e.g.
challenging and questioning	truancy
talking with teachers	refusal to comply
involvement in school councils	anti-social behaviour
campaigns, petitions, etc.	opting for another school

constructive ———————————————————————— destructive

e.g.	e.g.
regular attendance	mistrust of school and teachers
speaking well of the school	casual misuse of environment
showing respect to teachers	lack of engagement
acceptance of tasks	indifference to self as learner

LOYALTY	NEGLECT

passive

Figure 4.1 Dimensions of disaffection
Source: adapted from Lyons and Lowery (1986:331)

of parents responding to their own and/or their child's dissatisfaction by seeking to transfer her or him to another school. But that, of course, is not an option that is universally available.

Neglect as a passive/destructive form of response Neglect is destructive in that it involves a withdrawal into alienation, cynicism and distrust. Students whose response to disaffection falls into this category are likely to be mistrustful of their schools and teachers and to show little or no regard for the physical environment of the school. Their engagement with classroom tasks will be minimal and they will show a marked indifference to themselves as learners. While none of the categories are gender-specific, research suggests that male students are more likely to be neglectful in their expressions of disaffection and female students to be loyal. It also suggests that the often implicit messages given by the verbal and non-verbal behaviour of teachers in the classroom reinforce these tendencies:

'female students are nudged into passivity, dependency, and silence rather than activity, autonomy and talk' (LaFrance 1991:10).

Loyalty as a passive/constructive form of response   The loyalty form of response entails passively waiting for conditions to improve or simply accepting with a good grace that they never will. Loyalty in most institutions is seen as a virtue. In schools this is particularly so, since the loyal student invariably attends regularly, speaks well of the school, shows respect to teachers and accepts without question tasks that are set. What the model highlights, however, is the strong element of passive compliance that may be implicit in these supposedly desirable student behaviours. Schools that accept at face value the loyalty of their students make life that much easier for themselves, but arguably at the expense of the active engagement and participation by students in their own learning.

Voice as an active/constructive form of response   Voice involves an effort by students themselves to improve the conditions giving rise to their own disaffection. This would include students challenging and questioning teachers regarding tasks set, talking with teachers and tutors about progress, involving themselves in school councils and forums, and possibly organizing petitions and campaigns. The important point to note is that, in many schools, the kinds of behaviour that fall into this category are seen as either disruptive or as tending towards disruption. To see such behaviour in positive terms requires of teachers immense commitment and is extremely demanding of their time and of their organizational skills.

The meaning of membership: the school as a community of difference

The model briefly outlined above highlights the need for schools to encourage students to adopt those attitudes and behaviours that lie towards the active and constructive ends of the two intersecting continua and to refuse an easy trade-off between compliance and passivity. What our experience of the learning school teaches us is that new forms of partnership are required if young people are to be encouraged to participate actively and constructively in their own learning. The learning school is centrally concerned with membership, and membership must include parents and the community if the problems of disaffection – of estrangement and alienation – are to be acknowledged and a serious attempt made to resolve them. Through its acknowledgement and celebration of cultural diversity and its own commitment to work 'on the boundaries', the learning school reiterates in its management practices that principled

opposition to the tradition of 'selective differentiation' that is evident in its pedagogical, curriculum and assessment practices. It highlights the need for a sense of membership – of belongingness – that
is open and outward looking; inclusive and integrative.

A head teacher we spoke to offered a vivid depiction of the challenge and difficulty inherent in any attempt to create this sense of
belongingness:

> There are more than twelve major community languages spoken
> by the parents of children at this school. In some homes up to
> four languages are spoken. Many of our children are multi-
> lingual, although their amazing language skills go largely un-
> recognised because the languages they speak at home, or on
> the street, are not the languages that matter . . . There are also
> different religious groups and different groupings within the
> different religions. Each has its own beliefs and traditions . . .
>
> Our job is to bring this all together. Not by getting everybody
> to think in the same way, but by convincing everyone that
> learning matters. You know, most parents really want the best
> for their children. So it's not an impossible task. Most of them
> want their children to fulfil themselves, to take responsibility
> for their own lives. They wouldn't put it like that, of course,
> but it's there and it's our job, I think, to work with them, to
> help them define their own needs, to meet those needs . . . We
> can't do it on our own.

Community, it is often assumed, must be based upon similarity.
What the previous statement invites us to imagine, however, is another kind of community: one constituted around the recognition
of difference. Such a school acknowledges the experience of estrangement and alienation among students and parents and encourages
the active expression by them of their own feelings of disaffection;
it aspires to build open relationships between teachers, parents and
the community in such a way that the rights and responsibilities of
each are respected; it works with other schools to develop a coherent
and continuous system of educational provision; and, finally, it treats
the professional development and support of its own teaching staff
with great seriousness. It seeks an integrative mode of practice, not
only at the level of pedagogy, curriculum and assessment, but also
at the level of organizational structure:

Organizing for participation   The learning school seeks to involve
teachers, parents and the community in its values and vision. It
recognizes the reality of disaffection and seeks to create a climate

within which the causes of disaffection can be understood and confronted. The learning school confirms and extends the meaning of membership.

Organizing through dialogue The learning school requires a recognition of difference through open dialogue and discourse. It creates opportunities for individuals and groups to meet and talk about the ends and means of education. The organization of the learning school is itself implicated in the processes and procedures of learning.

Organizing through partnership The learning school brings together disparate groups to support and encourage learning. It provides a forum for the public discussion of educational values and purposes, a forum that includes students, teachers, parents and members of the local communities. The learning school locates itself 'on the boundaries'.

Organizing for life The learning school focuses on learning as a life-long process and on the need for close links between institutions. It operates according to an ethic of co-operation, not competition, and works closely with neighbouring schools and colleges. The learning school values continuity and progression and sees the student's quest for coherence as being of central importance.

FIVE

Towards the twenty-first century

In the opening chapter of this book we argued that the alternative reform agendas of recent years have failed to grasp the magnitude of disadvantage or to understand the social, moral and political significance of change. Consequently, they have failed to offer a model of learning that is adequate to the transformations of our time and that matches the new kinds of problems we face. Chapter 2 set about the task of developing such a model: it defined learning in terms of agency and capacity and defined the influences operating upon learning in terms of institutional structure and cultural formation. Chapters 3 and 4 applied that model in analysing the institutional practices and organizing assumptions of schools in contexts of disadvantage. In this final chapter we seek to develop a vision of schools within a learning democracy which can realize the values that underpin our analytical model of learning.

Reconstructing agency

The central task of the learning school is the reconstruction of agency. The motivation young people need to sustain this reconstruction can only grow out of a sense of purpose, that the struggle to develop as a person has some point. The conditions for young people taking themselves and thus their learning seriously depend upon the school having the highest expectations of their potential – providing encouragement, believing in their capacities, and recognizing and valuing equally their different identities. In this way schools can transform the way young people think of themselves and what they are capable of achieving.

Celebrating capacity

What we achieve is always tied to the sense we have of ourselves as learners, and that sense of ourselves is often dependent upon the expectations others have of us. The confidence we have in ourselves and others have in us is also indissolubly connected to the circumstances in which we live. For it may be understandable that those who live with too little to eat, in damp housing and with recurrent sickness may find the rigours of learning more arduous than those who find themselves in more fortunate circumstances. Those who live in a different world of relative disadvantage may understandably find the purpose of learning hopeless and futile. Those, moreover, who find their identity and cultural traditions unacknowledged in school and community also may find it difficult to summon the necessary enthusiasm for their learning. The recognition of worlds of difference is essential for many young people to value themselves, and thus the purpose of their learning.

The relationship between what young people achieve and the social conditions in which they live is, according to all the research evidence, incontrovertibly strong (Halsey *et al.* 1980; Bourdieu 1977). Context shapes learning. The health of students and the cultural space which is made available will have a determining influence upon their capacity and motivation to learn. Growing up in such conditions which make learning an uphill struggle, young people will find it more difficult to succeed and will thus enter adult life with the same disadvantages that they began with which they will pass on to their own children. A cycle of deprivation continues. The stubborn trend is for society to reproduce its inherited pattern of advantage and disadvantage.

Education cannot repair the leaking roof, restore the broken marriage and the loss of parental support, or dissolve disease and ill-health. Only society can create 'a settlement for justice', as in 1945, to ensure that all citizens have a fair distribution of the primary goods and opportunities (Rawls 1971) which enable them to flourish. In that sense education, as Bernstein (1971) famously stated, cannot compensate for society. Schools may not have a responsibility, as one Glasgow primary head in the past understandably saw fit to take upon himself, to provide breakfast for those children who come to school without anything to eat. Working with the appropriate professional services, the necessary support may be able to be provided.

Yet education can make a difference to what young people achieve. School matters (Rutter 1979; Mortimore *et al.* 1988; Smith and

Tomlinson 1989). Good schools enable their students to achieve, to realize their potential, to develop confidence in themselves and their capacities. Education can make a difference to the expectations which underpin learning. It cannot immediately change society and it cannot do its work without understanding and engaging with the attitudes and beliefs which young people and their families bring to learning. Education, of all the public services, can seek to illuminate so as to dissolve the impact of those deep cultural processes of social classification which erect boundaries of inclusion and exclusion, of self and other.

The central task for our time is to challenge such classifications in order to transform the way people think of themselves and what they are capable of. It is only by changing the sense students have of themselves as learners that they will begin to develop their capacities and realize their potential. Some urban communities facing multiple deprivation have made this understanding central to their social and educational strategy: 'Something had to be done to remove the stigma and feeling of cynicism and hopelessness so evident on the estates'. The institutions which traditionally we have assumed to provide support for the disadvantaged are defined as part of the problem because of the way they 'operated to repress the hopes of ordinary people. The problem was essentially one of how people on low incomes were treated and made to see themselves and their capabilities – living down to other people's expectations'. Patronizing professional bureaucracies can burden rather than liberate the community's capacity for regeneration. Renewal cannot be imposed but can only grow out of the confidence the people have in their capacity to create a future for themselves.

It can be difficult for a professional community which is sensitive to the plight many young people face to expect them to transcend their circumstances given the energy and the resources which that implies. Yet recognizing the centrality of motivation to learning, unless teachers work closely and continuously with parents and the community to establish the expectations which provide the conditions for confidence and learning to flourish, then young people are likely to underachieve. Partnership between home and school is crucial to motivation. Educators cannot raise the drawbridge on their local communities and hope to succeed.

Schools must play a leading role in transforming the way young people think about themselves and their capacities so that they can actively contribute to the renewal of their communities as we move towards the twenty-first century. Fulfilling this agenda will, however, require a cultural shift in many schools, as well as in society, to recognize and value the culturally different identities which comprise them.

Valuing difference equally

The experience of prejudice and discrimination continues to damage the lives of too many in our society, producing despair as well as anger. Prejudice reflects a closed mind which fears difference. Where views about other people become fixed and unalterable, so that beliefs about them and what they do are always based upon the same preconceived attitudes, then it is appropriate to speak of prejudice, or 'pre-judgement' about the characteristics which people possess. The effect of prejudice is to stereotype the attributes and qualities which individuals or groups are supposed to possess in a preconceived way that appears unamenable to contrary experience or evidence or reasonable questioning (Swann 1985:13).

The social foundations and consequences of prejudice are the social practices of discrimination – the working of the closed society. The mental processes of stereotyping that which is different and unusual have their counterpart in the processes of social selection and exclusion. In many communities considerable pressures are placed upon their members to conform to social norms of belief and behaviour. Attempts made by individuals to break with convention can meet with ridicule or sanction while outsiders, whose culture may threaten accepted patterns, are excluded:

> There are enormous pressures to conformity, to conform to some social norm . . . There is cultural dominance in British society which picks out that which is alien in belief and behaviour and attacks it. Throughout our history there has been a language and culture which celebrates white, English, protestant, heterosexual males despite the existence of, and the exclusion of other groups in society. There is a putting forward, promoting of, one ideal of 'normality' which bears no relation to the population in the community.
>
> The key issue is to establish respect for difference. The fact that one is fat, or blind, or female, or have a different colour skin, or have a different sexual orientation should not be a cause for social abuse or exclusion.
>
> (London Action Group)

The moral imperative of our time is to learn to relate to people because of what they are in themselves as persons and as citizens rather than because of some extrinsic characteristic they happen to possess. The central challenge for education is to encourage in young people as well as in the community as a whole the commitment to question and to analyse prejudice so that critical reflection dissolves corrupted thinking. What is at issue is the right to be respected as a human being, in the same way that we have an obligation to respect others. Such mutuality provides the condition for individuals as well as communities to grow and flourish. The respect which I need from you to recognize my difference and uniqueness, I must in turn accord you for your difference. If I deny your difference while asserting my right to be treated as human I am drawn in to the same distorted thinking.

The essence of learning is the willingness to open up to new ideas, knowledge and experience; and to enter a culture is to begin to learn. Though to begin to learn requires one to recognize the significance of language and culture for one's own identity: 'We must challenge a school system which celebrates only one kind of culture.'

The first stage of according value and respect to a plurality of cultures is to develop a culturally diverse curriculum in schools. Many teachers are deeply committed to this principle: to reviewing their own practice and thus the language they use, the attitudes they express, their teaching style as well as the content of the curriculum and the books and materials used in the classroom. Many teachers are concerned to ensure their work represents all the cultural values and faiths of the children they teach:

> Culturally diverse education is about valuing others, understanding them, opening oneself up to other experiences and appreciating that people are not necessarily like you. This is the central theme of our work: each child is important – they have rights, qualities which are unique to them. And families are individual, unique – they have a sense of achievement which is unique to them. We concentrate on the positive. We try to get the children to recognize this in each other, the individuality in others whether in colour, race or sex. We use cultural artefacts to encourage the valuing of difference.

A number of schools have found the arts can be a vital way of helping young people to express their own cultural identities and yet to value others. The positive, non-judgemental atmosphere of creating music or drama encourages understanding of other cultures.

In setting itself against manifest inequality, the learning school is not searching for sameness. As Anne Phillips (1993:34) points out, 'unity premised on simple similarity can be powerful but in the end restrictive – attractive but in the end destructive. We are not all the same, and the pretence that we are will not help us to change the world.' Difference is a defining feature of the contexts of disadvantage with which we are concerned. It is not just that such contexts are culturally diverse, but that such diversity brings with it a plurality of values.

The central problem is how schools can respond positively to these different values: 'some particularist, some claiming a universal validity, but each rooted in different traditions, histories and theoretical and political trajectories, and many of them in stark contradiction, one to the other' (Weeks 1993:189). It is because schools are located within these interlocking pluralities that, as institutions, they have to go on learning. Also, as members of those institutions, teachers have to go on thinking through the importance of education as a means of opening up opportunities and ensuring that every child has access to as wide a range of cultural resources as possible.

Values are important, not because they provide logical explanations, but because they are asserted and require assent. They affect action by satisfying our sense of what feels right or awakening our sense of what is morally offensive. The affective nature of values – the way they cling to feelings and associations – accounts for their resilience and for the continuing influence they exert across generations. Values take us, as individuals and groups, back to our roots for the purpose of reclaiming what is morally alive in our communal pasts; they trace old loyalties, but point also to new possibilities for realizing our own moral agency and for supporting that of others. They can, and do, lead to the exclusivity of tribal and ethnic nationalisms, but are also expressed in innumerable acts of individual altruism and self-sacrifice. 'The history of cultures and social formations is', as John Fekete (1988:i) reminds us, 'unintelligible except in relation to a history of value orientations, value ideals, goods values, value responses, and value judgements, and their objectivisations, interplay, and transformations.' Values are what make our various worlds go round.

The problem, then, is not simply one of culture clashes, between, say, school and home or school and community. How can the school, as a community of teachers and learners, grasp learning as a necessary condition of living together in an increasingly complex and fragmented world? How, in other words, can learning be seen, not as just another value position to set alongside – and against – all the others, but as a means of bringing together pluralities of value within a coherent frame of discourse and practice? Conceived in these terms, learning is not so much the old ivory tower as a new kind of meeting place characterized by the recognition of, and respect for, difference.

This position is by no means easy to sustain. In the 'real' world, values are almost invariably evoked in order to be promoted in their own right or defended against the encroachment of other values. The value of education, however, is of a very different order. It is concerned, not with interlocking sets of dichotomies by which oppositional attitudes and responses become a necessity, but with the shared experience of moral complexity. This concern for communality – for ways of living together with intelligence and mutual understanding – defines whatever it is that is educational about education. For learning to live together in a morally complex world is also, necessarily, a matter of learning to learn together.

The challenge is not to tolerate difference but to recognize and reaffirm it. As Anne Phillips (1994:79) points out, toleration is a poor substitute for recognition: 'We only tolerate what we do not like or approve of (otherwise there is no need for toleration), and yet where difference is bound up with identity, this is hard for the tolerated to accept.' The denial of cultural difference compounds the problem of alienation and estrangement experienced by many young people: either it ghettoizes them within their own contexts of disadvantage or else it persuades them to reject their cultural origins altogether. In either case it fails them (although traditionally disadvantaged students who are persuaded to reject their own cultural origins are numbered among the education system's successes).

There is a third way which is part of a different tradition whereby schools are seeking to engage more fully with the complex processes of cultural reproduction. Within that tradition progress in learning is not dependent on what students jettison by way of their own cultural identities. It is a matter, rather, of how the student draws on her or his own identity to understand that of others. 'The problem, after all,' argues Anne Phillips (1993:160), 'is not just how to achieve a fairer distribution of resources and power between groups we expect to remain hostile, or contemptuous of one another. The problem is how to generate that more comprehensive understanding that validates the worth of each group.'

For schools that are trying to seriously address the agency of the learner, progress in learning is necessarily integrative and cumulative in respect of cultural difference. It involves valuing individuals equally but also valuing the differences within and between communities.

Learning to learn in the learning school

If the learning school is to reconstruct both the sense of agency amongst young people and their capacity to make the communities in which they are to live, then many schools will have some fundamental relearning to do. They must learn to value and celebrate the capacity and culturally diverse identities of all their young citizens as the precondition for creating the motivation to learn. If schools are to realize this ambition they will have to learn about how they work as organizations, bringing to the surface the deep categories which typically selectively differentiate what they expect different young people to achieve. Schools must become learning organizations if they are to enable the necessary cultural renewal of active citizenship.

Learning is a process of discovery about why things are as they are and how they might become. Such understanding grows from processes of reflection that reveal the connection between things which had previously been unrecognized or opaque. Discovery is most likely to occur through experience, when people immerse themselves in the practice of activities so that their meaning becomes transparent. Once the working of a particular system has been revealed, it then becomes amenable to change, and it is the experience of change that provides the catalyst to learning. Knowledge only lives and has meaning through action. This 'action learning' perspective has been applied to modern organizations by Revans (1982) and Handy (1989) for whom a theory of learning is also a theory of changing. Learning implies understanding that will lead into action and that ongoing practice will be transformed as a result.

The significance of these learning processes for organizations, as well as for individuals, and the conditions which enable learning have become a distinctive tradition of study. The nature of the learning organization has been explored in different sectors: in health (Attwood and Beer 1988; Harrow and Willcocks 1990, 1992); in planning (Friedmann 1987); in education (Holly and Southworth 1989); and in business (Pedler *et al.* 1991; Lessem 1993). A distinctive framework for analysing the learning organization has become influential in this literature.

Loops of learning

In 1978, Argyris and Schön (see Argyris 1993) introduced an important distinction between levels of complexity in processes of learning: single and double loop learning. In single loop learning a simple change is made to an activity which is not working effectively. For example, within an incremental budgeting system, overspend could be corrected by reducing the level of increment to each service. Double loop learning questions the underlying assumptions which inform the activities, in this case perhaps reviewing the principles on which budgets are constructed.

> Single loop learning is like a thermostat that learns when it is too hot or too cold and turns the heat on or off. The thermostat can perform this task because it can receive information (the temparature of the room) and take corrective action. Double loop learning occurs when error is detected and corrected in ways that involve modification of an organisation's underlying norms, policies and objectives.
>
> (p.34)

Certain problems cannot be resolved without reflecting back on the very principles which inform practices and which are usually taken for granted. Argyris and Schön believe that whereas most organizations do quite well at the simpler learning, they have great difficulties in the more complex double loop learning. This is because many organizations are predisposed to inhibit processes of reflection which bring into question fundamental objectives and beliefs.

What are the conditions for learning?

Different kinds of learning, Argyris and Schön argue, require different conditions. Simple problems can be resolved by forms of inquiry which enable new information to come to the surface, or connections to be made within an activity which had not hitherto been appreciated, but the recognition of their interdependence is essential for effective action to proceed. In these inquiries certain processes are vital for their success: the value placed upon questioning to elucidate information, clarity of ideas, testing ideas against the evidence, and building up patterns or trends of activity. It is helpful to perceive these learning processes as a cycle (see Kolb 1984; Revans 1982; Handy 1989).

Figure 5.1 shows how learning starts with curiosity about a particular problem or puzzle which issues in questions to be answered. These we describe as triggers for learning. The inquiry stimulated by such triggers leads us to form ideas or conjectures or theories about what causes the problem, and then to test these ideas. Deliberation

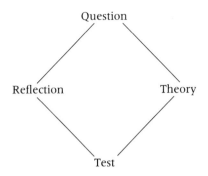

Figure 5.1 The learning cycle

on the experience can illuminate the underlying processes and produce learning which changes the way we arrange an activity. It might even change the way we think about the activity or lead us to new activities.

The source of some problems, however, lies in the differences of perspective or belief which individuals or groups within an organization may have and which may prevent them reaching agreement about what counts as evidence or a relevant question. Understanding falls down because of the failure of communication: individuals cannot understand each other because they do not grasp the meaning and significance of the other's concepts. The solution depends upon the willingness of groups to listen to opposing interpretations and reach agreement about a new framework of values and assumptions. For many organizations, however, the reality of conflicting perspectives may not be recognized or be actively suppressed. Organizations may need to develop skills in conflict management. The task is to create the conditions for double loop learning:

> the consequence of learning should be an emphasis on double-loop learning, by means of which individuals confront the basic assumptions behind the present views of others and invite confrontation of their own basic assumptions, and by which underlying hypotheses are tested publicly and are made disconfirmable, not self-sealing.
>   . . . an enhancement of the conditions for *organisational* double-loop learning, where assumptions and norms central to organisational theory-in-use are surfaced . . . publicly confronted, tested and restructured.
>
>   (Argyris and Schön 1978:139)

In the right conditions, people can react in different ways, so that they are more amenable to the difficult processes of questioning their own beliefs and becoming more receptive to the value of others' beliefs: if double-loop learning is to occur: people would

- feel less defensive
- feel free to take risks
- each person would search for his inconsistencies and encourage the other to confront them
- both would be able to state their views in ways that are disconfirmable
- both would believe that public testing would not be harmful.

The conditions that are most appropriate to supporting double loop learning are those which reinforce open discussion in search of agreement. Such a context mirrors within the organization Habermas's (1984) conditions for communicative rationality, in which speakers in public strive to make claims which are true, correct and sincere. When committed to these principles speakers are orientated to correct mistaken perceptions and to synthesize perspectives when rationally possible: 'the correction of . . . errors requires the conditions of the good dialectic, which begins with the development of a map that provides a different perspective on the problem (e.g. a different set of governing values or norms). The opposition of ideas and persons then makes it possible to invent responses that approximate the organisation's espoused theory' (Habermas 1984).

The struggles between groups present dilemmas for organizations, but also opportunities when they can lead into double loop learning, because it can enable an organization to unify around shared purposes. But the dialectic which prepares for any such synthesis of perspectives may not be an easy process:

The good dialectic . . . is not a matter of smoothness of operation or elimination of error. On the contrary, its goodness is inherent in the ways in which error is continually interpreted and corrected, incompatibility and incongruity are continually engaged, and conflict is continually confronted and resolved . . . the dialectical process focuses attention on incompatibility of norms and objectives which are not resolvable by a search for the most effective means. For norms set the criteria by which effectiveness may be judged.

(Habermas 1984)

Learning to learn

The most effective process of learning is learning how to learn. Organizations experiencing change need a general predisposition to learn if they are to succeed. Bateson (1973) has called this 'deutero-learning', in which individuals become creative at learning about how they have been learning: they reflect on and analyse their previous styles of learning or failing to learn. They clarify what enabled or blocked their learning so that they can take remedial action and develop new strategies for learning. In organizations, Argyris and Schön propose, the new strategies become encoded in mental maps that reshape organizational practice: learning continually questions the *status quo*, the theories in use. People have to learn how to learn, discover how to discover, invent, generalize, learn how to establish a good dialectic (Argyris and Schön 1978).

The learning organization becomes self-aware about the cycles of learning and the conditions for learning. It becomes proficient at asking questions, developing ideas, testing them and reflecting on practice.

Awareness of the cycles of learning encourages participants to explore continually the conditions of learning, why it is that individuals and groups are open to new ideas, new ways of thinking which keep them at the front end of change. Learning pushes back the boundaries of inquiry about the conditions which support and constrain change, laying bare the deep structures of social action. The individual explores the constraints and opportunities of the organizational context in which she works; while the organization similarly questions the limits of the wider society in which it is located. Learning continually extends the cycle of learning.

In this way the learning process explores the structures of action: the values which underlie the perspectives, the forms of interaction and the nature and distribution of power that drives action. Learning about these systems of action within organizations is best nurtured within 'action learning sets' that enable the participants, through collaborative working and reflection, to open out to and accommodate the value in each perspective and to develop the predisposition to change practice. The capacity for learning is the capacity for dialectic in changing practice.

Unless schools develop the qualities of the learning organization then their capacity to lead the reconstruction of agency and contribute to the learning society will be considerably reduced. A learning organization will be more likely to engage in an internal discourse – able to challenge its deep-seated assumptions about 'ability' – if it is located within, and part of, an active democratic public domain (Ranson and Stewart 1994). The organizing principles of that domain are principles for learning, which must involve double loop learning, that can challenge existing organizations and activities. That will be achieved by open public discourse which is not bounded by existing activities. The process of discourse in the public domain is the basis for learning to learn.

Schools within and for a learning democracy

The renewal our society is looking for to sustain it into the twenty-first century will depend upon a cultural shift in favour of a learning society which celebrates the purposive nature of being and the creative contribution which citizens can make to the well-being of all. The discussion has sought to articulate the purposes and conditions which can support the unfolding of learning for active citizenship and emphasized the significance of motivation for learning. Such motivation requires encouragement, resources and, most importantly, the valuing of the different (cultural) identities which young people bring to learning. The learning school can create the internal discourse that challenges taken-for-granted assumptions about identity and capacity. A flourishing public domain provides the necessary conditions by making such a dialogue about the value of different identities public and democratic.

We can only make ourselves and our communities when empowered by a discourse that recognizes the distinctive contributions each has to contribute. Such a discourse will depend upon the existence of a strong, participatory democracy which legitimates and values politics, because it is only through such a system of governance that people can constitute the conditions for making a life that:

- acknowledges their values
- recognizes their differences
- accords them identity
- sustains the material conditions of existence.

The different purposes can only be developed and reconciled through a discourse which alone can constitute how we are to agree a future, and which can also connect a personal morality with a just polity to indicate how we are to live together. The conditions for learning lie in motivation and the conditions for motivation have their roots in a participative democracy. This understanding can best unfold when learning is conceived as supported by a local institutional and democratic system of education. We develop this concluding argument in stages.

Learning is inescapably a system   learning is a process which cannot be contained within the boundaries of any one institution. Discovery and understanding occur at home, in the community, on a scheme of work experience as well as in college or school. Progress, furthermore, will unfold more securely between stages of learning when they are mutually comprehending and supporting. Improving achievement depends for its realization upon enabling a wider system of learning: one element cannot be treated in isolation from another if each is to contribute to the effective working of the whole. Ensuring that every school has the appropriate numbers of pupils and the sufficient provision of resources and teachers to support a balanced and comprehensive curriculum with choices at key stages to enable progression in response to diversity of need is a task which has to be managed at the level of the system as a whole, as well as the school, if all young people are to be provided with opportunities to realize their powers and capacities.

Learning needs to be managed as a local system   the system of learning is more effective if managed locally, as well as nationally and at the level of the institution. The different tasks need their appropriate tier of management. The conditions for excellence in local education require the strategic leadership which a local system of education management can provide. Such a local system is needed to ensure understanding of local needs, responsiveness to changing circumstances, and efficiency in the management of resources within geographic boundaries consistent with identifiable historical traditions. Such local systems need to be properly accountable and this requires location within a local democratic system.

Learning needs to be supported within a local democratic system   the quality of learning, however, is not only dependent upon the effectiveness of the local system of management, but also, crucially, upon the wider local political system in which it is located. Learning, as we have argued, will depend upon parental and community involvement as well as the strength of the wider public domain.

Parents need to be closely involved with schools and working in partnership with teachers to support the learning process. The evidence suggests that where this happens the motivation of young people is considerably enhanced, and this leads to significant improvement in achievement. It is, in part, because parents are so significant an influence upon the quality of achievement that institutions and the wider education service need to reach out to develop parents' understanding of the many and varied innovations in curriculum and teaching over recent years. If parents are to fulfil their appropriate role as complementary educators then they need to make sense of learning strategies; this requires professionals to learn to work in partnership with parents, governors and the community.

While professionals need to learn to communicate the meaning and purpose of new practice, they also need to listen. The best teachers know that by working with and listening to parents they can develop an understanding of language and culture that can provide the key to the progress of particular pupils.

This significance of parents to learning, however, illustrates the necessary rights of parents to be involved in the school and the education system. Parents have a right to be:

• valued
• informed about the school and their child's achievement
• involved in decisions about their child's education
• involved in school activities
• involved in the learning process as complementary educators.

The participation of parents, many believe, can help break the cycle of underachievement in education. The partnership with parents is increasingly recognized as essential to motivating and reinforcing the achievement of the young learner. Parents are valued as complementary educators and encouraged to become learners themselves. Being involved in the learning process will raise the awareness of adults themselves about their own educational needs and personal development.

For many parents who have had little involvement in education or sympathy with it, involving them in the educational process in a non-threatening and supportive way could have a positive spin-off in the quality of life and direct educational benefit for parents themselves. We have had parents involved informally in home–school link schemes who begin to realize the gaps in their own education and have gone on to take up courses: the involvement has begun to lift their aspirations.

When parents experience educational achievement it creates positive reinforcement for them, strengthens their self-image and confidence. 'They realize they have got skills and abilities to offer their children, which they did not think they had. This developing awareness of skills and how to use them for their children is

the outstanding feature'. Enabling self-confidence and celebrating
achievement of parents will also reinforce their motivation and ability to contribute to the quality of life in the community.

By creating achievement, education helps adults as well as young
people to develop the capacities and confidence to make a wider
contribution to their community, and thus invests lives with meaning and purpose. The learning school will look beyond the boundary
of the institution and be committed to support learning within the
wider community, recognizing its indirect benefit for young people
but also valuing the extension of education for its own sake. The
learning process is not confined to the classroom, nor what is taught.
When schools acknowledge that learning continues throughout life
they will begin to recognize the learning needs of others in the
community and make their provision more flexible in order to meet
the needs of the community as a whole.

The learning school understands that developing a neighbourhood as a whole is the precondition for regenerating highly disadvantaged communities. Only by improving the quality, resources
and capacity of the community will it be able to improve the quality
of life for all, hence the importance of rebuilding the confidence
and fulfilling the potential of all the people within the community. A community development perspective can achieve this. It will
improve the quality of life: involving the community will improve
the confidence, performance and effectiveness of its members. It
will develop the resources and capacities of individuals and thus
improve the quality of life for all.

The school in the learning society seeks to use its understanding
and resources wherever possible to support education across the
community. It perceives local shops and offices, community centres
and clubs as providing opportunities for learning. A model for
such developments is often available in the voluntary sector where
centres offer educational activities for the community: playgroups,
classes for adults, art classes for pensioners, drama for disabled
children. The knowledge and advice within the professional institution becomes available to support and enrich the wider community:
language skills, careers advice, outreach work to discover educational
needs in the community.

Most importantly, young people grow up learning their responsibilities as citizens, to understand and serve the needs of others in
the community. This orientation, together with the active curriculum, is providing young people with a richer vision of the purpose
of learning. Thus the Glasgow secondary school committed to the
recovery of the waste land and the glen wood was encouraging

young people to develop the understanding and capacities to create a sustainable environment. While they were enacting their formal curriculum – whether it be the history of the area, or wildlife studies in biology, or the environmental sciences, or in re-creating local stories, or in the performance arts – they were breathing in a hidden curriculum of learning to make and to take responsibility for their local communities.

The argument so far supports the participation of parents and members of the community as learners and complementary educators because it enhances the learning society. Education, however, is always a public good as well as a personal benefit. Even if learning is considered an experience of individuals alone it will, through its enhancing of capacities, always have a wider significance which properly concerns the whole community. The need to develop the community as a whole, as much as the powers and capacities of each, makes education properly a service of and for the commonwealth. It is this inescapable characteristic of the service which requires the participation of the public as citizens as well as clients.

Thus people need to be involved collectively as well as individually in influencing the development of what is essentially a public service, the characteristics of which cannot be determined by individuals acting in isolation from each other. The quality of education therefore requires to be the subject of public choice which is accountable to the public as a whole.

If choice is to be public choice it requires the opportunity for citizens to express their view, for their voice to be heard, so that the inescapably diverse constituencies of education are enabled to present, discuss and negotiate their account. Public choice presupposes public participation and mutual accountability:

> The deliberative process of democratic decision-making requires that each participant not only permit the others to express their views and offer their judgements but take others' views seriously into account in arriving at his or her own judgement. Clearly this does not require agreement with the views of others, but rather serious attention to, and respect for, their views. Such reciprocal respect also presupposes that disagreements be tolerated and not suppressed.
>
> (Gould 1988)

Such an active citizenship requires the necessary conditions for participation: extensive consultation, the use of surveys as well as using the authority's outreach staff to listen to the views of the public. Community polling could be another approach to encouraging public choice. A constitutive condition, however, for any citizenship is to provide arenas for active public participation. By providing forums for participation, the new polity can create the conditions for public discourse and for mutual accountability so that citizens can take each other's needs and claims into account and will learn to create the conditions for each other's development. Learning as discourse must underpin the learning society as the defining condition of the public domain.

A model in the recent past has been the creation of local youth councils which have enabled young people to debate and make decisions about youth policy and provision. Some schools have developed community councils which involve a broader representation than formal governing bodies in order to make the life of the school wherever possible serve the needs of the community as a whole as well as parents. Some colleges have sought to play an enabling role with community businesses by providing the community with skills, advice and resources to deploy as they choose. The role of the educator is to encourage community groups to take responsibility and ownership for their own learning enterprise.

An education service which seeks actively to involve citizens in policy-making and to become accountable to the community as a whole needs to constitute local community forums or councils. These would enable several interests – including women's groups, the black and ethnic minorities and the disabled – within a community to participate, articulate needs and contribute to decision-making. Where an authority has formed a pool of resources – perhaps from urban aid funds, EU or local grants – to support community groups, decision-making about distribution could be delegated to these forums. In this way citizens within the community are being enfranchised to influence and take responsibility for their own learning environment. They can negotiate with the providers to use educational resources so as to meet the learning needs of the community as a whole: in access courses, 'women back to work' classes, health courses, community languages, bilingual learning and so on.

Yet these developments presuppose the prior existence and pre-eminent significance of local government in and for education. Such initiatives to extend and improve participation of citizens in public services builds upon and requires the institutions of local democracy. Participation is needed to complement representation in the evolution of local government. The more immediate arenas of personal participation need to be underwritten and informed by the institutions and legitimacy of the council chamber and its public committees. In this way a more elaborate political system is developed which enables a wider public debate about the purpose and process of education, about

- the learning needs of individuals and groups
- the rights and entitlements of the disadvantaged
- complaints and injustice
- ideas for improving the quality of service delivery.

Such a system would encourage public choices which were more responsive to the community as a whole and thus based upon consent. At the same time it would hold services more accountable to the public.

The local education authority, therefore, is an institution of local democracy as well as a framework for managing the system to enhance the quality of learning. Its essential purpose, as well as its capacity to enable educational achievement, derives from this source. By unfolding capacities for responsible autonomy and choice, an education generates the value as well as the conditions for living in a democracy; while an accountable democracy – through its traditions of public discourse – is the only means of ensuring an education worth having.

Education and local democracy are thus mutually reinforcing: their purpose is one and the same – a learning society. Developments which have become preconditions for the educational progress of many young people – a gender-neutral curriculum, bilingual teaching, multicultural education, comprehensive schooling – emerged, not from Whitehall, nor from isolated individuals but instead from discourse, local democracy and public action.

Conclusion

There is no solitary learning: we can only create our worlds together. The unfolding agency of the self always grows out of the interaction with others. It is inescapably a social creation. We can only develop as persons with and through others; the conception of the self presupposes an understanding of what we are to become and this always unfolds through our relationship with others. The conditions in which the self develops and flourishes are social and political. The self can only find its identity in and through others and membership of communities. The possibility of shared understanding requires individuals not only to value others but to create the communities in which mutuality and thus the conditions for learning can flourish. The telos of learning is to learn to make the communities without which individuals cannot grow and develop.

The values of the learning society, enabling all people to make a purpose of their lives, can create the conditions for motivation in the classroom. A learning society would encourage individuals to value their active role as citizens and thus their shared responsibility for the commonwealth. Active learning in the classroom needs, therefore, to be informed by and lead towards citizenship within a participative democracy. Teachers and educational managers, with their deep understanding of the processes of learning, can, we believe, play a leading role in enabling such a vision to unfold not only among young people but also across the public domain.

References

Archer, M. (1979) *Social Origins of Educational Systems*. London: Sage.

Argyris, C. (1993) *On Organisational Learning*. Oxford: Blackwell.

Argyris, C. and Schön, D. (1978) *Organisational Learning: A Theory of Action Perspective*. London: Addison-Wesley.

Attwood, M. and Beer, N. (1988) Developments of a learning organisation, *Management, Education and Development*, 19(3).

Ball, S. (1993) Education markets, choice and social class: the market as class strategy in the UK and USA, *British Journal of Sociology of Education*, 14(1):3–19.

Bateson, G. (1973) *Steps to an Ecology of Mind*. London: Paladin.

Bauman, Z. (1973) *Culture as Praxis*. London: Routledge and Kegan Paul.

Bauman, Z. (1992) *Intimations of Postmodernity*. London: Routledge.

Bernstein, B. (1971) Education cannot compensate for society, in B.R. Cosin *et al.* (eds) *School and Society: A Sociological Reader*. London: Routledge and Kegan Paul in association with the Open University.

Bernstein, B. (1975) *Class, Codes and Control: Volume 3 Towards a Theory of Educational Transmissions* (revised edition). London: Routledge and Kegan Paul.

Bolton, E. (1992) Speech to National Commission on Education Conference in Shrewsbury. (Unpublished.)

Bourdieu, P. (1977) *Outline of a Theory of Practice*. Cambridge: Cambridge University Press.

Bourdieu, P. (1990) *The Logic of Practice* (trans. R. Nice). Cambridge: Polity.

CCCS (1978) Social democracy, education and the crisis, Occasional Paper No.52, Birmingham, Centre for Contemporary Cultural Studies.

Chandler, A.D. (1962) *Strategy and Structure*. Cambridge, MA: MIT Press.

Channel Four Commission on Education (1991) *Every Child in Britain* (Report of the Channel Four Commission on Education). London: Channel Four Television.

Commission on Social Justice (1994) *Social Justice: Strategies for National Renewal* (Report of the Commission on Social Justice). London: Vintage.

Dahrendof, R. (1994) The changing quality of citizenship, in B. van Steen-bergen (ed.) *The Condition of Citizenship*. London: Sage.

Davies, R.P. (ed.) (1975) *Mixed-Ability Grouping*. London: Temple-Smith.

DE (1943) *Educational Reconstruction* (White Paper), Cmd 6458. London: HMSO.

Dearing, R. (1993) *The National Curriculum and its Assessment: An Interim Report*. London: National Curriculum Council/School Examinations and Assessment Council.

Dearing, R. (1994) *The National Curriculum and its Assessment: Final Report*. London: School Curriculum and Assessment Authority.

Department for Education (1992) *Choice and Diversity: A New Framework for Schools* (White Paper). London: HMSO.

Department of Education and Science (1967) *Children and their Primary Schools* (The Plowden Report). London: HMSO.

Department of Education and Science (1976) *The Yellow Book*. Unpublished, but in DFE library.

Department of Education and Science (1977) *Education in Schools: A Consultative Document* (Green Paper). London: HMSO.

Department of Education and Science (1985a) *General Certificate of Secondary Education: The National Criteria: General Criteria*. London: HMSO.

Department of Education and Science (1985b) *Better Schools*, Cmd 9469. London: HMSO.

Department of Education and Science (1991) *Education and Training for the Twenty-first Century*. London: HMSO.

Douglas, J.W.B. (1964) *The Home and the School*. London: MacGibbon and Kee.

Dunn, J. (ed.) (1992) *Democracy: The Unfinished Journey*. Oxford: Oxford University Press.

Echols, F., McPherson, A. and Willms, D. (1990) Parental choice in Scotland, *Journal of Education Policy*, 5(3):207–22.

Eggleston, S.J., Dunn, D.K. and Anjali, M. (1986) *Education for one: the Educational and Vocational Experiences of 15–18 Year Old Members of Minority Ethnic Groups*. Stoke-on-Trent: Trentham.

Eliot, T.S. (1948) *Notes Towards the Definition of Culture*. London: Faber and Faber.

Fekete, J. (1988) Introductory notes for a postmodern value agenda, in J. Fekete (ed.) *Life After Postmodernism: Essays on Value and Culture*. London: Macmillan.

Friedmann, J. (1987) *Planning in the Public Domain: From Knowledge to action*. Princeton, NJ: Princeton University Press.

Gadamer, H.G. (1975) *Truth and Method*. London: Steed and Ward.

Gardner, H. (1983) *Frames of Mind*. New York: Basic Books.

Gardner, H. (1985) *The Mind's New Science*. London: Harper Collins.

Gellner, E. (1994) *Conditions of Liberty: Civil Society and its Rivals*. London: Hamish Hamilton.

Giddens, A. (1977) *Studies in Social and Political Theory*. London: Hutchinson.

Giddens, A. (1984) *The Constitution of Society: Outline of the Theory of Structuration*. Cambridge: Polity.

Giddens, A. (1991) *Modernity and Self-Identity: Self and Society in the Late Modern Age*. Cambridge: Polity.

Giddens, A. (1992) *The Transformation of Intimacy: Sexuality, Love and Eroticism in Modern Societies*. Cambridge: Polity.

Gilligan, C. (1986) Remapping the moral domain, in T. Heller, M. Sosna and D. Wellbury (eds) *Reconstruction of Individualism: Antonamy, Individuality and the Self in Western Thought*. Stanford, CA: Stanford University Press.

Gould, C. (1988) *Rethinking Democracy: Freedom and Social Cooperation in Politics, Economy and Society*. Cambridge: Cambridge University Press.

Gray, J. (1993) *Beyond the New Right: Markets, Government and the Common Environment*. London: Routledge.

Habermas, J. (1984) *The Theory of Communicative Action. Volume 1: Reason and Rationalisation of Society*. London: Heinemann.

Hall, S. (1990) Cultural identity and the diaspora, in J. Rutherford (ed.) *Identity: Community, Culture, Difference*. London: Lawrence and Wishart.

Halsey, A.H., Heath, A.F. and Ridge, J.M. (1980) *Origins and Destinations: Family, Class and Education in Modern Britain*. Oxford: Oxford University Press.

Handy, C. (1989) *The Age of Unreason*. London: Arrow.

Hargreaves, D. (1984) *Improving Secondary Schools*. London: Inner London Education Authority.

Hargreaves, D. (1994) *The Mosaic of Learning: Schools and Teachers for the Next Century*. London: Demos.

Harrow, J. and Willcocks, L. (1990) Public services management: activities, initiatives and limits to learning, *Journal of Management Studies*, 27(3).

Hart, S. (1992) Differentiation. Part of the problem or part of the solution?, *The Curriculum Journal*, 3(2):132–42.

Her Majesty's Senior Chief Inspector (1990) *Standards in Education 1988–89* (Annual Report of HM Senior Chief Inspector). London: HMI/DES.

Her Majesty's Senior Chief Inspector (1991) *Standards in Education 1989–90* (Annual Report of HM Senior Chief Inspector). London: HMI/DES.

Hirschman, A.O. (1970) *Exit, Voice and Loyalty: Responses to Decline in Firms, Organizations, and States*. Cambridge, MA: Harvard University Press.

Holly, P. and Southworth, G. (1989) *The Developing School*. London: Falmer.

Institute for Public Policy Research (1993) *Education: A Different Vision (An Alternative White Paper)*. London: Institute for Public Policy Research.

Jackson, B. (1964) *Streaming: An Education System in Miniature*. London: Routledge and Kegan Paul.

Jonathan, R. (1989) Choice and control in education: parental rights, individual liberty and social justice, *British Journal of Educational Studies*, 37(4):321–38.

Joseph Rowntree Foundation (1995) *Inquiry into Income and Wealth*. York: Joseph Rowntree Foundation.

Kelly, A.V. (1974) *Teaching Mixed Ability Classes*. London: Harper and Row.

Kelly, A.V. (ed.) (1975) *Case Studies in Mixed Ability Teaching*. London: Harper and Row.

Kelly, A.V. (1978) *Mixed Ability Grouping: Theory and Practice*. London: Harper and Row.

Keys, W. and Fernandes, C. (1993) *What Do Students Think About School?* Slough: NFER.

Kolb, D. (1984) *Experiential Learning*. Englewood Cliffs, NJ: Prentice Hall.

Labour Party (1994) *Opening Doors to a Learning Society: A Policy Statement on Education*. London: The Labour Party.

LaFrance, M. (1991) School for scandal: different educational experiences for females and males, *Gender and Education*, 3(1):3–13.

Lessem, R. (1993) *Business as a Learning Community*. London: McGraw-Hill.

Lowery, D., DeHoog, R.H. and Lyons, W.E. (1992) Citizenship in the empowered locality: an elaboration, a critique and a partial test, *Urban Affairs Quarterly*, 28(1):69–103.

Lyons, W.E. and Lowery, D. (1986) The organisation of political space and citizen responses to dissatisfaction in urban communities: an integrative model, *Journal of Politics*, 48(2):321–46.

Lyons, W.E. and Lowery, D. (1989) Citizen responses to dissatisfaction in urban communities: a partial test of a general model, *Journal of Politics*, 51(4):841–68.

Lyons, W.E., Lowery, D. and DeHoog, R.H. (1992) *The Politics of Dissatisfaction: Citizens, Services, and Urban Institutions*. New York: M.E. Sharpe, Inc.

MacIntyre, A. (1981) *After Virtue: A Study in Moral Theory*. London: Duckworth.

Mortimore, P., Sammons, P., Stoll, L., Lewis, D. and Ecob, R. (1988) *School Matters: The Junior Years*. Wells, Somerset: Open Books.

National Commission on Education (1993a) *Learning to Succeed* (Report of the Paul Hamlyn Foundation National Commission on Education). London: Heinemann.

National Commission on Education (1993b) *Briefings*. London: Heinemann.

National Commission on Education (1994) *Insights into Education and Training* (Papers collected by the Paul Hamlyn Foundation). London: Heinemann.

National Curriculum Council (1989) *Circular Number 6*. York: National Curriculum Council.

Nussbaum, M. (1990) Aristotelian social democracy, in G. Mara and H. Richardson (eds) *Liberalism and the Good*. New York: Routledge.

Okin, S.M. (1991) Gender, the public and the private, in D. Held (ed.) *Political Theory Today*. Cambridge: Polity Press.

Parfit, O. (1984) *Reasons and Persons*. Oxford: Clarendon.

Pateman, C. (1987) Feminist critiques of the public/private dichotomy, in A. Phillips (ed.) *Feminism and Equality*. Oxford: Basil Blackwell.

Pedler, M., Burgoyne, J. and Boydell, T. (1991) *The Learning Company*. (London: McGraw-Hill).

Peters, R.S. (1966) *Ethics and Education*. London: George, Allen and Unwin.

Phillips, A. (1991) *Engendering Democracy*. Cambridge: Polity.

Phillips, A. (1993) *Democracy and Difference*. Cambridge: Polity.

Phillips, A. (1994) Dealing with difference: a politics of ideas or a politics of presence, *Constellations*, 1(1):74–91.

Rampton, A. (1981) *West Indian Children in our Schools* (Interim Report of the Committee of Inquiry into the Education of Children from Ethnic Minority Groups) (the Rampton Report). London: HMSO.

Ranson, S. (1992) Towards the Learning Society, *Education Management and Administration*, 20(2).

Ranson, S. (1993) Markets or Democracy for Education, *British Journal of Education*, 41(4):333–52.

Ranson, S. (1994) *Towards the Learning Society*. London: Cassell.

Ranson, S. and Stewart, J. (1994) *Management for the Public Domain: Enabling the Learning Society*. London: Macmillan.

Rawls, J. (1971) *A Theory of Justice*. Oxford: Clarendon.

Revans, R. (1982) *The Origins and Growth of Action Learning*. Bromley: Chartwell Brett.

Robbins, L. (1963) *Higher Education* (The Robbins Report) Cmnd 2154. London: HMSO.

Rutherford, J. (ed.) (1990) Identity: *Community, Culture, Differences*. London: Lawrence and Wishart.

Rutter, M., Maughan, B., Mortimore, P. and Ousten, J. with Smith, A. (1979) *Fifteen Thousand Hours: Secondary Schools and their Effects on Children*. Shepton Mallet: Open Books.

Ryan, A. (1974) An essentially contested concept. *Times Higher Educational Supplement*, 1 February.

Secondary Examinations Council (1985) *Working Paper 1: Differentiated Assessment in GCSE*. London: Secondary Examinations Council.

Sharp, E. (1984a) Exit, voice, and loyalty in the context of local government problems, *Western Political Quarterly*, 37:67–83.

Sharp, E. (1984b) Citizen demand making in the urban context, *American Journal of Political Science*, 28:654–70.

Shotter, J. (1993) *Cultural Politics of Everyday Life: Social Constructionism, Rhetoric and Knowing of the Third Kind*. Buckingham: Open University Press.

Simpson, M. and Ure, J. (1993) *What's the Difference? A Study of Differentiation in Scottish Secondary Schools*. Dundee: Northern College Publications.

Smith, D.J. and Tomlinson, S. (1989) *The School Effect: A Study of Multi-Racial Comprehensives*. London: Policy Studies Institute.

Steiner, G. (1971) *In Bluebeard's Castle: Some Notes towards the Re-definition of Culture*. London: Faber and Faber.

Swann (1985) *Education for All* (Report of the Committee of Inquiry into the Education of Children from Ethnic Minority Groups) (the Swann Report). London: HMSO.

Weeks, J. (1990) The value of difference, in J. Rutherford (ed.) *Identity: Community, Culture, Difference*. London: Lawrence and Wishart.

Weeks, J. (1993) Rediscovering values, in J. Squires (ed.) *Principled Positions: Postmodernism and the Rediscovery of Value*. London: Lawrence and Wishart.

Weston, P. and Barrett, E. with Jamison, J. (1992) *The Quest for Coherence: Managing the Whole Curriculum 5–16.* Slough: NFER.

Williams, R. (1963) *Culture and Society 1780–1950.* Harmondsworth: Penguin association with Chatto and Windus. (First published in 1958 by Chatto and Windus.)

Williams, R. (1965) *The Long Revolution.* Harmondsworth: Penguin (first published by Chatto and Windus, 1961).

Williams, R. (1977) *Marxism and Literature.* Oxford: Oxford University Press.

Williams, R. (1980) *Problems in Materialism and Culture.* London: Verso.

Wragg, E.C. (ed.) (1976) *Teaching Mixed Ability Groups.* London: David and Charles.

Index